STUDIES ON THE RESURRECTION OF CHRIST

COMPILED BY HAYES PRESS

Copyright © Hayes Press 2015

All rights reserved. No part of this book may be reproduced, stored in a retrieval system, or transmitted in any form, without the written permission of Hayes Press.

Published by:

HAYES PRESS Publisher, Resources & Media,

The Barn, Flaxlands

Royal Wootton Bassett

Swindon, SN4 8DY

United Kingdom

www.hayespress.org

Unless otherwise indicated, all Scripture quotations are from the HOLY BIBLE, the New King James Version® (NKJV®). Copyright © 1982 Thomas Nelson, Inc. Used by permission. All rights reserved. Scriptures marked NIV are from New International Version®, NIV® Copyright © 1973, 1978, 1984, 2011 by Biblica, Inc.™ Used by permission. All rights reserved worldwide. Scriptures marked NASB are from the New American Standard Bible®, Copyright © 1960, 1962, 1963, 1968, 1971, 1972, 1973, 1975, 1977, 1995 by The Lockman Foundation. Used by permission (www.Lockman.org).

CHAPTER ONE: INTRODUCTION (TOM HYLAND)

At the basis of the Christian Faith lies the glorious fact of our Saviour's triumphant resurrection from the dead on the third day. This is the culminating event recorded in each of the four Gospel narratives and it is attested by indisputable evidence. It is supported by the united testimony of the apostles, and when it became necessary to nominate another to take the place of Judas, Peter stipulated that he must be one who had companied with the twelve throughout the Lord's ministry until the day He was received up into heaven. "Of these," said Peter, "must one become a witness with us of His resurrection" (Acts 1:22). And the apostle Paul, also, in reply to critics of his apostolic authority, wrote, "Am I not an apostle? Have I not seen Jesus our Lord?" (1 Corinthians 9:1).

The resurrection of Christ became the cornerstone in the preaching of the apostles. There can be no question as to the importance they attached to this unparalleled event of which they had first-hand knowledge. A study of their recorded addresses in Acts shows the extent to which their preaching was influenced by their absolute certainty that there was a risen Saviour in heaven (see e.g., Acts 2:24; 4:10; 5:30,31; 17:31; 26:23). The apostle Paul describes the raising of Christ from the dead, and His exaltation to God's right hand in heaven, as the supreme example of divine power (Ephesians 1:19-23), and emphasizes in unqualified terms the cruciality of the resurrection, in the well-known passage: "If Christ hath not been raised, then is our preaching vain, your faith also is vain ... ye are yet in your sins ... If in this life only we have hoped in Christ, we are of all men most pitiable" (1 Corinthians 15:14-19).

Resurrection has to do with the body, and the bodily resurrection of Christ is clearly stated both in the Gospels and the Epistles. Each of the Gospels records the burial of Christ and asserts that the tomb was empty when visited and examined by witnesses, early on the third day His body was buried and His body was raised. In the light of the elaborate precautions taken to guard the tomb, the failure of the Jews to produce the body speaks for itself. Our Lord appeared to His apostles in bodily form after His resurrection and showed them His wounded hands feet and side This is clear evidence against those who teach that our Lord's resurrection was spiritual and not physical It is true that His body underwent some change in, its properties, nevertheless, the body that came from the Virgin's womb was the body that was buried in Joseph's tomb and restored to life.

Undoubtedly, the resurrection of Christ is the greatest miracle of all. Beside it all other miracles pale. The claims Christ made for Himself were unique, and during His lifetime those claims were amply supported by His words and by His works. His death, too, was unique. No mere man could have died as He died. "Truly this man was the Son of God" was the verdict of the Roman centurion who observed the Saviour's conduct throughout the hours He hung upon the Cross. But the resurrection is the crowning proof of His deity: He "was declared to be the Son of God with power, according to the spirit of holiness, by the resurrection of the dead" (Romans 1:4). No further proof is necessary.

Our Lord was "raised on the third day according to the Scriptures" (1 Corinthians 15:4). His resurrection was planned by God and foretold in the Old Testament writings. The testimony of prophecy to this great event was acknowledged and emphasized by our Lord himself. He came to fulfil the Scriptures and His resurrection was an essential part of that fulfilment. And not only is there direct prophecy to this great truth, but it is also concealed in many of the types and shadows of the Old Testament. Throughout these writings there are many references to the glories which should follow the sufferings of the Christ. On this theme the prophets loved to dwell as the Spirit of Christ which was in them pointed forward to the glorious triumph over sin and death of the Redeemer who was to come.

During our Lord's public ministry, as recorded in the Gospels, He revealed that He would be set at naught and crucified, but that He would be raised from the dead on the third day. So open was His claim that He would rise again from the dead that His enemies were fully informed of it. After His crucifixion they said to Pontius Pilate, "Sir, we remember that that deceiver said, while He was yet alive, after three days I rise again. Command therefore that the sepulchre be made sure until the third day" (Matthew 27:63,64). Their testimony to our Lord's prediction of His own resurrection and the steps they took to nullify His words are confirming evidence from hostile witnesses. As opposition mounted and rejection by the rulers became increasingly apparent, the Cross cast its shadow across our Lord's path. But never in His mind was the suffering of death divorced from the triumph of resurrection. On the Mount of Transfiguration, the coming glory was glimpsed, and coming down from the mount the Lord commanded, "Tell the vision to no man, until the Son of Man be risen from the dead" (Matthew 17:9).

His ministry to His apostles was now concentrated on the fulfilment of the great purpose of God in His death and resurrection (Matthew 16:21). This accumulation of prediction to the resurrection of Christ, by prophecy and type in the Old Testament, by the open testimony of our Lord during His ministry, which was confirmed by His enemies, and by the emphasis He gave to it in His closing ministry to His apostles, is conclusive evidence of its centrality in God's purposes.

The resurrection of Christ, then, is a fact of history firmly established on unassailable evidence. But the evidence is by no means exhausted when we have established its historicity. Its reality and power are endorsed in human experience to a degree which cannot be disregarded. The impact of the resurrection on the apostles was transforming. The crucifixion had left them in a state of abject fear. When the reality of the resurrection was grasped by them they became as bold as lions. Clothed with power from on high, "with great power gave the apostles their witness of the resurrection of the Lord Jesus" (Acts 4:33). Threats, persecution, and imprisonment failed to intimidate them. The boldness of Peter and John astounded the council before whom they were arraigned. "We cannot", they said, "but speak the things which we saw and heard" (Acts 4:20).

Could there be more convincing evidence of the transforming power of the resurrection than the conversion of Saul of Tarsus? What could account for the turnabout of this bigoted Pharisee but his confrontation with the risen Lord? "Last of all", the apostle testified, "He appeared to me also. For I am the least of the apostles, that am not meet to be called an apostle" (1 Corinthians 15:8,9). Millions since that day have believed although they have not seen, but their contact with the risen Lord is witnessed by the transformation of their lives. "I got a glimpse of One", wrote Joseph Barker, late infidel lecturer, "on whom it is impossible to look without experiencing transformation of soul." The certainty of this experience is well expressed in the lines:

We know the Son of God has come,

We know He died and rose,

We know He liveth now

At God's right hand above,

We know the throne on which He sits,

We know His truth and love.

Add the testimony of human experience to the historical record and the truth of the resurrection is placed beyond question. "The Lord is risen indeed!" (Luke 24:34) was the triumphant exclamation on that first Lord's day. The Father waited to welcome His conquering Son and, in glorified humanity, the Son took His place at the Father's right hand. Satan was defeated, God was vindicated, Christ was victorious, heaven was opened. The Holy Spirit was sent to garner the harvest which would follow the Redeemer's death. Our Lord's mysterious reference to death and resurrection now became meaningful: "Verily, verily, I say unto you, except a grain of wheat fall into the earth and die it abideth by itself alone; but if it die, it beareth much fruit" (John 12:24).

Wonderful is the fact of our Lord's resurrection; still more wonderful are its consequences. At His incarnation our Lord took human nature into deity; at His resurrection He took manhood into heaven. He did not assume manhood merely for the period of His earthly sojourn and then lay h aside. When He ascended where He was before to take His place at the right hand of the Father He did so in His glorified human body. Thus, He is "the Firstborn from the dead" (Colossians 1:18), and "the Firstfruits of them that are asleep" (1 Corinthians 15:20). The presence of one glorified Man in heaven is the guarantee of a mighty harvest to follow. His death and resurrection have secured for all the redeemed a glorified bodily nature like His: He "shall fashion anew the body of our humiliation, that it may be conformed to the body of His glory, according to the working whereby He is able even to subject all things unto Himself" (Philippians 3:21).

The First begotten from the dead,

He's risen now, His people's Head,

And thus their life's secure.

And if like Him they yield their breath,

Like Him they'll burst the bonds of death,

Their resurrection sure.

Thus the historical fact of the resurrection of Christ became a basic doctrine of the Christian Faith. It signified the acceptance by God of the Saviour's atoning death: "Jesus our Lord … who was delivered up for our trespasses, and was raised for our justification" (Romans 4:24-25). Moreover, the resurrection ensured union with Christ. The believer becomes united to Christ by indissoluble bonds. As mankind are "in Adam" and share the consequences of Adam's sin, so believers are "in Christ" and share in Christ's life and righteousness. Thus they are eternally secure. The second Man can never fail.

In the epistles the resurrection of Christ is also viewed in relation to the believer's present life and conduct. What should be the impact of the resurrection in terms of present-day Christian experience? This is, perhaps, a neglected area in New Testament studies, but it was a vital and practical element in apostolic teaching. One of the great truths they emphasized was that of our identification with Christ. His death and resurrection were our death and resurrection. We died with Him and we have been raised with Him: "God ... raised us up with Him, and made us to sit with Him in the heavenly places, in Christ Jesus" (Ephesians 2:4-6). Thus the believer really belongs to the heavenly sphere while he still lives on earth. Some of the tensions of the Christian life arise from this dual relationship. But this wonderful truth of our identification with the risen Christ is associated with the power for victorious Christian living. What God has done with us should have corresponding results in us. See how Paul reasons this out in the passage Romans 6:4-14. This seems to be related to his own great longing that he might "know Him, and the power of His resurrection" (Philippians 3:10).

"Rooted in the deep realities of the regenerate existence and the spiritual consciousness, and having essential associations with the inward things of grace, the resurrection is with Paul not simply an objective event, a destiny to be looked for, a new condition to be anticipated, but an attainment, an object of aspiration and strenuous moral endeavour, to be reached only by suffering loss, by being found in Christ, by knowing Him in the power which He has over us and in us in virtue of His resurrection, by partnership with Him in suffering, by becoming conformed unto His death and dying as He died unto sin" (Salmond).

We are persuaded that this truth of our identification with Christ and its possibilities in terms of Christian living are of greater consequence than is generally recognized. We have sketched roughly some of the ground which can be explored in the consideration of this great subject of the resurrection of our Lord Jesus Christ. Various writers have undertaken to deal in more detail with different facets of the subject. We trust that this book will confirm faith and encourage the practical application to ourselves of the possibilities embodied in this fundamental doctrine of the Christian Faith.

CHAPTER TWO: PREDICTED IN OLD TESTAMENT PROPHECY (GEORGE PRASHER JNR.)

"Who hath declared it from the beginning, that we may know?" (Isaiah 41:26).

This forceful challenge through the prophet Isaiah illustrates one of God's ways in revelation. Long beforehand He declared certain of His great purposes, so that when they came to pass they could be clearly recognized as His work. Isaiah repeatedly called upon false claimants to spiritual revelation to do what Jehovah did through his prophets: "Declare the things that are to come hereafter, that we may know that ye are gods" (Isaiah 41:23).

There was, of course, nothing comparable to the foreknowledge of Israel's God, who in this as in all else was uniquely exalted far above all: "I am God, and there is none else; I am God, and there is none like Me; declaring the end from the beginning, and from ancient times things that are not yet done; saying, My counsel shall stand, and I will do all My pleasure ... I have purposed, I will also do it" (Isaiah 46:9-11).

Among the greatest purposes of our God stands the resurrection from among the dead of His beloved Son. Known in eternal counsels, this dramatic secret was in due course foretold by the divine Spirit through God's holy prophets. It was imparted to them a whole millennium before the morning when the stone was rolled away to reveal that Christ's tomb was empty. The prophets themselves would doubtless read repeatedly what they had written under the constraint of the Spirit, "searching what time or what manner of time the Spirit of Christ which was in them did point unto". However limited their own appreciation of the resurrection of the Messiah, these prophecies are to us in retrospect brilliant gems of revelation, aglow with assurance of truth; the truth of the most crucial fact in history, the event upon which our hopes for eternity are based.

On the surface of the Old Testament prophetic word there are rich allusions to the sufferings of Christ and the glories that should follow them. These prophecies are especially prominent in the writings of David and Isaiah. In the 22nd Psalm David poignantly describes the anguish of the Crucified. What believer has not been led with chastened spirit to view again the sufferings of Calvary in the light of Isaiah 53? Yet in these passages David and Isaiah are both led forward from the pathos of Messiah's suffering to the glories of His exaltation. What does this imply? Nothing less than the bringing again from the dead of the great Shepherd of the sheep!' There is writ large over a wide area of Old Testament prophecy the truth of the Sufferer become triumphant, a seeming paradox which finds its solution in His resurrection from the dead. Two illustrations of this, Psalms 110:1 and 118:22, are taken up by the apostle Peter in Acts 2:34 and 4:11 in order to confirm by the Old Testament word the resurrection of the Lord Jesus.

Unaided we might have overlooked the implication of the prophet's words in Isaiah 55:3, had not the Spirit of God drawn attention to them in Paul's ministry at Antioch: "As concerning that He raised Him up from the dead, now no more to return to corruption, He hath spoken on this wise, I will give you the holy and sure blessings of David" (Acts 13:34).

By this we are reminded of the need to search carefully in the Old Testament prophetic word for references to the resurrection of the Lord Jesus. Had we been favoured to company with the two on the way to Emmaus as the Lord interpreted to them in all the Scriptures the things concerning Himself, it is probable that many passages formerly overlooked would have shone with new light as pointing forward to that mighty event. For example, is the deliverance described in Psalm 18:7-19 confined to some experience in David's life? Does not this immense movement in divine power point to an event transcending anything that David ever needed or knew? Does it not foretell "that exceeding greatness of His power", "that working of the strength of His might which He wrought in Christ, when He raised Him from the dead, and made Him to sit at His right hand in the heavenly places?" (Ephesians 1:19-20). Again in the 85th Psalm, of the sons of Korah, if verse ten so concisely outlines the great moral truths of reconciliation at Calvary, does not verse eleven foretell the bursting forth of truth on the resurrection morning, despite all the vain attempts of Jewish intrigue and Roman power to "hold down the truth in unrighteousness"? Similarly may we not hear the voice of the Spirit as to the Lord's resurrection in the plaintive appeal of the prophet Hosea (6:1-2)? If this portion appears to be isolated in context from other references to the Lord Jesus, the marvel of the prophetic element is enhanced. Such is the sovereign working of the Lord, the Spirit.

Without question David was inspired of God to foretell the resurrection of the Lord Jesus in the last four verses of the sixteenth

Psalm. This remarkable prophecy was quoted by Peter on the day of Pentecost (Acts 2:25-28) in confirmation of the fact that the Lord had been raised from the dead. Demonstrating that David could not have written about himself, for he died, was buried, and his tomb could still be seen in Jerusalem at that time, Peter proceeded to declare: "Being therefore a prophet ... he foreseeing this spake of the resurrection of the Christ, that neither was He left in Hades, nor did His flesh see corruption" (verses 30,31).

Quoting from the same Psalm in Antioch of Pisidia, Paul reasoned in similar strain: "For David, after he had in his own generation served the counsel of God, fell on sleep, and was laid unto his fathers, and saw corruption: but He whom God raised up saw no corruption" (Acts 13:36-37).

This Psalm stands as a landmark of prophetic truth in relation to the resurrection of the Lord Jesus. It declared the fact of the resurrection one thousand years before the event took place. With marvellous brevity it distinguished between the condition of the Lord's soul and body during the interval between death and resurrection. For the Lord's body was to be with the rich in His death, in the fresh coolness of a new tomb "where never man had yet lain", preciously answering to the emptying of ashes from Old Covenant offerings in a clean place (Leviticus 4:12). In that tomb the body of our Saviour saw no corruption. His soul was in that part of Hades (or Hell) where saints of past ages reposed (Luke 16:23), awaiting the moment of liberation and triumph on the first day of the week. Looking back in the light of New Covenant revelation we recognize these truths 'to have been enshrined in David's Spirit-directed words: "Thou wilt not leave

My soul to Sheol, neither wilt Thou suffer Thine Holy One to see corruption."

How wonderfully such prophets "spake from God, being moved by the Holy Spirit"! For to a certain extent the sixteenth Psalm may be read as an expression of David's own experiences (e.g. verses 1-7). Yet he was guided in later verses to write, although still in the first person, of something entirely beyond his own experience. Such is one of the prophetic forms of Old Testament revelation, causing us to bow in adoration at the ways of God in using human instruments to convey His thoughts and purposes in Christ.

In relation to the resurrection of the Lord Jesus, then, "we have the word of prophecy made more sure; whereunto ye do well that ye take heed, as unto a lamp shining in a dark place, until the day dawn, and the day-star arise in your hearts" (2 Peter 1:19). For ten centuries before the great day of His resurrection the prophetic lamp of Old Testament prophecy shone undimmed regarding this event. To the believer's heart it shines on with reassuring clarity in a world of spiritual darkness which would wish to disprove the evidence of the empty tomb.

"Thy testimonies are wonderful ... the opening of Thy words giveth light; ... Of old have I known from Thy testimonies, that Thou hast founded them for ever" (Psalm 119.129,130,152).

CHAPTER THREE: PICTURED IN OLD TESTAMENT TYPES (GEORGE PRASHER SNR.)

The resurrection of Christ as recorded in the four Gospels is a story of absorbing interest. It is also of vital consequence, because Christ's sacrificial death would have been of no avail had it not been followed by His triumphant resurrection. Our hearts, therefore, rejoice as we read Paul's assuring words: "But now hath Christ been raised from the dead, the firstfruits of them that are asleep" (1 Corinthians 15:20).

The theme of this chapter, however, is Christ's resurrection as seen in the types of the Old Testament. The history recorded in the Old Testament Scriptures is wonderful from the point of view that it gives not only the train of events in those early days, but also contains shadows or types of what would happen in days then in the distant future. Of the Book of Genesis it has been stated, "There is no doctrine of Christianity, however advanced, which is not found, at least in outline, there. It contains the germ of every future truth."

Let us look at some of the stories of this Book; firstly, that of the Flood in the days of Noah. He built an ark at the bidding and under the direction of God. This was for the salvation of himself and his house, together with the creatures which God directed into the ark. Man's dreadful guilt, whereby the earth became corrupt and was filled with violence, caused God to come in judgement, and for a period of many days the waters increased and prevailed until they rose above the highest mountains some fifteen cubits. This indicates the universality of the Flood. Then God remembered Noah, and every living thing with him in the ark, and made a wind to pass over the earth, and the waters assuaged, with the ark resting on the mountains of Ararat in the seventh month, on the seventeenth day of the month.

What is the significance of the Holy Spirit giving us the month and the day that the ark came to rest on the resurrected earth? Surely it is to link it with the fact that this day and month agrees with the day and month of the resurrection of the Lord Jesus Christ. The seventh month of the secular year became, at the time of Israel's redemption, the first month of the sacred year: "This month shall be unto you the beginning of months: it shall be the first month of the year to you" (Exodus 12:2). Christ our Passover was slain on the fourteenth day of the month, and three days after this, the seventeenth, He arose a Victor over the powers of Hell.

The story of Abraham offering up Isaac has shadows of the resurrection. Isaac's birth was a miracle, and his father loved him dearly; yet God called him to offer in sacrifice his son, his only son, whom he loved, even Isaac. Here is shadowed the activity of the Father and the Son whom God sent to be the Saviour of the world. The hand of Abraham, however, was stayed while the knife was raised to slay, and Isaac was released from the altar, a substitute being found in the ram that was caught in the thicket by his horns. The Holy Spirit's comment on this in Hebrews 11:19 is relevant: "Accounting that God is able to raise up, even from the dead; from whence he did also in a parable receive him back." Another translation of this verse is, "Hence he did get him back, by what was a parable of the resurrection."

Before passing from Genesis we may refer briefly to the account of Joseph. His life was commendable before God, and points to the greater than Joseph, the Lord Jesus Christ. Though Joseph had pleased God in his service, yet through the sin of his brothers on the one hand, and the wickedness of Potiphar's wife on the other hand, he was thrust down into the dungeon. Like the great Antitype he was suffering for sins not his own. The butler who had heard good news from Joseph went back to the palace, only to forget his benefactor. But God did not forget.

Through a dream that troubled Pharaoh, Joseph was summoned to the court, and after interpreting the dream was honoured by Pharaoh, who said, "Can we find such a one as this? ... Thou shalt be over my house, and according unto thy word shall all my people be ruled: only in the throne will he be greater than thou ... And they cried before him, Bow the knee: and he set him over all the land of Egypt" (Genesis 41:38-43). The seven steps of the Lord Jesus from the throne in heaven down to the cross on Golgotha, as recorded in Philippians 2, verses 7 and 8, are followed by exaltation. "Wherefore also God highly exalted Him, and gave unto Him the name which is above every name: that in the name of Jesus every knee should bow ... and that every tongue should confess that Jesus Christ is Lord, to the glory of God the Father." The resurrection came between the humiliation and the exaltation, as Joseph's exaltation was preceded by his ascending from the prison house.

In God's dealings with Israel, further shadows can be traced. Jacob went down to Egypt with his family. In number they were some 70 souls. There they multiplied and became a mighty nation. They were, however, in cruel bondage and servitude. God commissioned Moses and Aaron to go to Pharaoh and say, "Thus saith the Lord, Israel is My son, My firstborn: and I have said unto thee, Let My son go, that he may serve Me; and thou has refused to let him go: behold, I will slay thy son, thy firstborn" (Exodus 4:22, 23). So Moses and Aaron came to Pharaoh, "And they said, The God of the Hebrews hath met with us: let us go, we pray thee, three days' journey into the wilderness, and sacrifice unto the Lord our God" (5:3).

God terms Israel His son, His firstborn, thus giving us a shadow of Christ. The three days' journey into the wilderness indicates death, burial and resurrection. Death when the lamb was slain, and the firstborn of Egypt died; burial when the people passed through the sea, and the cloud was overhead; resurrection when they emerged on the wilderness side of the sea. Here they beheld their enemies dead upon the shore, and victory in resurrection is portrayed. The defeat of the enemy was overwhelming. "Then sang Moses and the children of Israel this song unto the Lord, and spake, saying, "I will sing unto the Lord, for He hath triumphed gloriously: the horse and his rider hath He thrown into the sea."

In Leviticus 14:7 we have a further type of Christ in resurrection. For the cleansing of the leper two living clean birds were brought. One was killed in an earthen vessel over running water. The blood was sprinkled on the leper, and the living bird was dipped in the blood of the bird that was killed. Then the priest let go the living bird into the open field. As it rose heavenward bearing the stains of blood it prefigured Christ who rose from the dead, and through His own blood entered in once and for all into the holy place, having obtained eternal redemption (Hebrews 9:12). So we rejoice and say, "Unto Him that loveth us, and loosed us from our sins by His blood ... be the glory and the dominion for ever and ever. Amen" (Revelation 1:5,6).

"Ye shall bring the sheaf of the firstfruits of your harvest unto the priest: and he shall wave the sheaf before the LORD, to be accepted for you: on the morrow after the sabbath the priest shall wave it" (Leviticus 23:10,11). This sheaf spoke of Christ in resurrection. We should note the words, "on the morrow after the sabbath".

That was the first day of the week, and was the day of the week when the Lord left the grave. "When the sabbath was past, Mary Magdalene, and Mary the mother of James, and Salome, bought spices, that they might come and anoint Him (Jesus). And very early on the first day of the week, they came to the tomb when the sun was risen" (Mark 16:1,2). They found the stone rolled back, and they entered the tomb, thereupon a young man arrayed in a white robe said to them, "He is risen; He is not here: Behold, the place where they laid Him!" He charged them to go and "tell His disciples, and Peter, He goeth before You into Galilee: there shall ye see Him, as He said unto you" (verse 7).

Galilee was a despised place, and it is still true that He is to be found among those whom the world despise. When they met Him there He gave commandment to go "and make disciples of all the nations, baptizing them into the name of Father and of the Son, and of the Holy Spirit: teaching them to observe all things whatsoever I commanded you: and lo, I am with you alway, even unto the end of the world" (Matthew 28:19,20). Those loyal to the risen Lord still gather on the first day of the week (Acts 20:7) to wave Christ before God-the Christ in whom we find acceptance.

We make one more reference to resurrection in shadow as seen in Jonah the prophet. The Lord Jesus said, "An evil and adulterous generation seeketh after a sign; and there shall no sign be given to it but the sign of Jonah the prophet: for as Jonah was three days and three nights in the belly of the sea-monster; so shall the Son of man be three days and three nights in the heart of the earth" (Matthew 12:39,40 RV margin). When Jonah went and preached to Nineveh the preaching that God had bidden him he was like a resurrected man. In the sign of Jonah the prophet, God spoke to the men of Ninevah, and they repented of their evil. They also received mercy and were saved from judgement. The three days and three nights which the Lord spent in the heart of the earth are also a sign which God expects man to accept. The promise is, "Because if thou shalt confess with thy mouth Jesus as Lord, and shalt believe in thy heart that God raised Him from the dead, thou shalt be saved" (Romans 10:9).

To summarize - in the Ark on Mount Ararat God is pointing to the day and month of Christ's resurrection; in Isaac we see somewhat of the love and affection which exist between the Father and the Son whom He raised from the dead; in Joseph it is the honour, power and authority which are Christ's in resurrection; at the Red Sea there is victory in resurrection, with rejoicing and praises to God through the overwhelming defeat of the enemy; in the living bird stained with the blood of the victim, and soaring upward, it is the cleansing power of the blood of Christ who in resurrection entered the holies in heaven through His own blood; in the wave sheaf it is Christ raised from the dead on the first day of the week, the Firstborn from among the dead; in Jonah we have a resurrected man with a message for sinners, prefiguring the Lord in resurrection whose message is forgiveness through faith in His name.

CHAPTER FOUR: PRESENTED IN THE LORD'S MINISTRY (BOB ARMSTRONG)

On the resurrection of the Lord Jesus Christ rests the whole work of redemption. Every promise God has given relative to the believer's life to come, depends on this great fact. Paul wrote to the church of God in Corinth, "But if there be no resurrection of the dead, then is Christ not risen: and if Christ be not risen, then is our preaching vain, and your faith is also vain ... And if Christ be not raised, your faith is vain; ye are yet in your sins ... If in this life only we have hope in Christ, we are of all men most miserable" (1 Corinthians 15:13-19 KJV). We purpose to look at the important statements made by the Lord Jesus in which He foretold His own resurrection from the dead.

During the silent years of our Lord's life, between the stirring days Luke describes, when His anxious parents found Him in the temple with the doctors of the law "both hearing them, and asking them questions", and His baptism by John in Jordan, He was aware of the great mission for which He had come to earth. It is marvellous to realize that as He grew up, "a tender plant" under the eye of God His Father, from Boyhood to young Manhood, He knew as Man what He already knew as God the Son in the eternal bosom of the Father. This is a great mystery.

In boyhood's holy days and in mature manhood, as He kept long prayer watches and pored over the Sacred Writings, the Holy Spirit opened His sinless mind to see the path of service, obedience and sacrifice He was to tread. Hebrews 5:8 tells us, "Though

He were a Son, yet learned He obedience by the things which he suffered".

David wrote, centuries before, that the Lord's consuming zeal for the house of God would make him virtually an outcast in His own home. "For Thy sake I have borne reproach: ... I am become a stranger unto My brethren, and an alien unto My mother's children. When I wept ... with fasting, that was to My reproach ... I became a proverb unto them. They that sit in the gate speak against Me" (Psalm 69:7-12). He was so totally different by the social standards of those days that He was unacceptable even to His own relatives. The Lord Jesus was not afraid of anyone. He did not hesitate to speak out against the moral and religious evils of His time. Although He was marked for death by the rulers because He dared to expose their wickedness, He knew He was right, but He also knew that His death and resurrection would come only at the appointed time, and by a voluntary act in keeping with His Father's will. As He looked across the dark valley of His sufferings and death, He saw the power and glory of His resurrection. It was to Him as though the sun of that glorious day had already risen, to shed its eternal rays on His completed work (Hebrews 12:2). So He looked forward to the joy set before Him, prepared to lose to gain, to die to live, to suffer to reign. Unlike men who know nothing of tomorrow's events, Christ knew the time and occasion of every step He would take.

The earliest reference made directly by Lord Jesus to His death and resurrection was shortly after His first miracle at the Cana wedding feast. He had just dealt with those traders in oxen and sheep and doves, and with the money-changers, who were making His Father's house a house of merchandise, and in answer to

His astounded observers who asked about His authority to do these things, He said, "Destroy this temple, and in three days I will raise it up" (John 2:19).

He had already shown His creative authority in changing water into wine, and His corrective authority in cleansing the temple, and if the people did not understand these, they were certainly at a greater loss to know what He meant by His redemptive authority, veiled in those remarkable words, and He made them none the wiser. Even His disciples did not understand until after He was raised from the dead. It was not the time to speak about the supreme events towards which He was quickly moving, and the record indicates He eventually told only His disciples. He made another reference to His resurrection just prior to the raising of Lazarus, "No man taketh it (My life) from Me, but I lay it down of Myself. I have power to lay it down, and I have power to take it again. This commandment have I received of My Father" (John 10:18).

Matthew 16.21, Mark 8.31, and Luke 9.22 all refer to the time when the Lord Jesus finally told His disciples that he would he killed, and "be raised the third day". He now began to speak plainly about His coming death and resurrection. These coming events of such great moment were hidden from the rulers and the people, and revealed to His disciples. As these words first fell on the dull minds of the disciples, even they could not understand why the Man they had left all to follow should anticipate death at such an early age; and the rising from the dead was even a greater mystery (Mark 9:10). They rather looked for deliverance and an earthly kingdom, and to be awarded places of honour at His right hand.

Peter, in a well-meaning attempt to preserve His Master's life, dared to rebuke the Lord, saying "Be it far from Thee, Lord: this shall not be unto Thee" (Matthew 16:22). Peter said, in effect, "Save Thyself," or "Have mercy on Thyself", Christ saw Satan in Peter that day. What could be more appealing to physical senses than to avoid a collision with mortal suffering, for the Lord well knew the terrible sufferings He would endure! Satan used the over-protectiveness of Peter, who seemed to assume the role of the Lord's personal bodyguard on occasions, but our Lord quickly recognized it as a trap or stumbling-block, to turn Him aside from the experience of Calvary. The Lord's words must have seared the very soul of Peter that day, but the issues were too vital to be trifled with. How solemn for Satan to be seen in a disciple, and yet how often it has been the case! Peter must often have thought of that day, when afterwards he stood out fearlessly and preached Jesus and the resurrection.

The Lord's path narrowed, as the crowds no longer followed Him, to touch Him or hear Him speak. He withdrew Himself and set a steadfast course to Jerusalem and Calvary. A noticeable change came over the Lord's countenance as He neared the time of His death and went with the disciples on what proved to be the last journey to Jerusalem. We read, "And they were in the way going up to Jerusalem; and Jesus went before them: and they were amazed: and as they followed, they were afraid". Here again the Lord confirmed the events of which He had spoken earlier.

"Behold, we go up to Jerusalem; and the Son of Man shall be delivered unto the chief priests, and into the scribes; and they shall condemn Him to death ... they shall mock Him, and shall scourge Him, and shall spit upon Him, and shall kill Him: and the third day He shall rise again" (Mark 10:32,24). He was a Man of singular purpose, nothing turned Him aside from the supreme objective of His life, to go through the experience of death and resurrection on which rests the vast plan of redemption.

The four Gospel writers make more than twenty references to the Lord's prediction of His own death and resurrection. His desire to have the disciples in full knowledge, if not the understanding, of these events, seems clearly to be linked with their call to apostleship and witnessing in after days. After He was raised from the dead, the things He had said to them were then clearly understood, and what power was theirs, in full possession of the fact of His resurrection: "and with great power gave the apostles witness of the resurrection of the Lord Jesus" (Acts 4:33).

It is instructive to notice that three Gospel writers record immediately following His statement concerning His approaching death and resurrection, the words of Christ about disciples bearing their own cross and following Him (see Matthew 16:24,25; Mark 8:34.35; Luke 9:23,24), "If any man will come after Me, let him deny himself, and take up his cross, and follow Me." Those disciples who closely follow the Lord will have the mark of death and resurrection upon them: "Dead indeed unto sin, but alive unto God through Jesus Christ". May it be so with each one of us!

It is obvious from the scriptures we have considered that neither the rulers nor the people knew the divine purpose behind the events surrounding the Crucifixion. Nor did they know that the body of this Man would be the first and only one in all history to lie in a tomb and be unaffected by the ravages of decay. Nor did anyone see in the darkness of that early morning a Figure suddenly move out from the shadows of death through sealed stone to the glorious path of resurrection. Yet its magnificent message has reached the four corners of the earth.

Up from the grave He arose,

With a mighty triumph o'er His foes;

He arose a Victor from the dark domain,

And He lives for ever with His saints to reign,

He arose! Hallelujah! Christ arose! (Robert Lowry)

CHAPTER FIVE: PORTRAYED IN THE GOSPELS (JAMES MARTIN)

As has been noted already, the Christian faith rests largely - we might almost say mainly - upon the doctrine of the Resurrection of the Lord Jesus Christ. The historical account of this great miracle is found in the four Gospels, respectively by Matthew, Mark, Luke, and John, supplemented by Peter and Paul in their writings. It is therefore important that we should ascertain if these records are reliable. This is a vast study in itself which has occupied historians, friendly and hostile, over many centuries, during which time more and more sources of evidence of the reliability of the New Testament records have come to light.

In assessing the trustworthiness of ancient historical writings one of the most important questions to be asked is, "How soon after the events were they recorded?" Evidence indicates that the first three Gospels, known as the Synoptic Gospels, are not later than circa A.D. 60, and that the latest of these was completed not much (if any) more than forty years after the death of Christ. Except in a prophetical way, there is no reference in any of these Gospels to the fall of Jerusalem, under Titus, which took place in A.D. 70.

During the last century, especially, the Gospel according to John has been the centre of many disputes. The author is "the disciple whom Jesus loved", an eyewitness of the events he records. From the places in John's Gospel where this description of the author appears (John 13:23; 19:26; 20:2) and other parallel scriptures in the Synoptic Gospels, it has been deduced, we believe rightly, that he was the apostle John. Of course, there are other internal evidences which lead to the same conclusion. With regard to the date, there is in the John Rylands Library, Manchester, a fragment of a papyrus codex of the fourth Gospel containing on the one side part verses 31 to 33, and on the other part verses 37 to 38 of chapter 18 of John's Gospel. Experts have dated this papyrus codex as circa A.D. 120. It is the earliest fragment, by at least fifty years, of the New Testament. By experts in this line of study, the date of the Gospel according to John has been placed between A.D. 90 and 100.

In agreement with one learned in this line of research, we quote: "We have good and sufficient grounds for accepting as valid for the whole Gospel by John the words of 19:35, which testify to the truth of the author's eyewitness report of the Lord's death, 'and he that hath seen bath borne witness, and his witness is true: and he knoweth that he saith true, that ye also may believe.'"

We turn now to the records of the Resurrection of the Lord in the four Gospels. Because of the vital importance of the fact of the Resurrection and all that depends thereon, it is not surprising that in all ages it has been vigorously assailed by sceptical writers. The central fact itself has been denied, and discrepancies in the various records have been suggested. Where one of the Gospel writers has not recorded any particular fact, the omission has been claimed as a denial of the statement made by others. Variations in description have been stated to be contradictions, even in cases where differences have in reality corroborated each other. A study of the four Gospels, even if we may fail to solve all difficulties and produce a perfect harmony, will reveal how the

Holy Spirit has anticipated the objections of sceptics. The believer in the Lord Jesus as his Saviour should have no difficulty in accepting the records in their full detail.

We propose to examine a few of these supposed discrepancies in the light of the inspired records. Some have claimed that the Lord did not actually die, but that He only swooned, and that in the cool tomb He recovered. His rising is claimed to be a resuscitation and not a resurrection. The words used in Scripture concerning the dying of the Lord by the four Evangelists are important. Matthew (27:50) writes that He "yielded up His spirit"; Mark (15:37) and Luke (23:46) record "gave up the ghost"; and John (19:30) records "gave up His spirit".

These words describe the voluntary dying of the Lord, words that could not be applied to the death of any mere human being. Further, the Roman soldiers, accustomed and hardened to crucifixion, saw that "He was dead already", therefore "they brake not His legs: howbeit one of them with a spear pierced His side, and straightway there came out blood and water" (John 19:31-37), another evidence of His death. Further still, two Sanhedrin counsellors of prominent estate, Joseph of Arimathea and Nicodemus, received the "corpse" from the centurion responsible for the crucifixion. Others also brought spices in addition to the hundred pounds provided by Nicodemus, and bound up the body in linen cloths. Surely we have here ample evidence of the death of the Lord.

A very powerful evidence of the Resurrection is the "empty tomb", concerning which there has been much disputation. To nullify the evidence of the bands of women who visited the tomb on the Saturday night and in the early hours of the first day of the week, it has been stated that they, in their grief, must have mistaken the exact location of Joseph's new tomb. Not so! Matthew (27:61) and Mark (15:47) tell us that Mary Magdalene and Mary the mother of Joses were there and they beheld (that is, carefully observed and took note) where He was laid. Whilst Luke (23:55,56) records that the other group, "the women, which had come with Him out of Galilee, followed after, and beheld the tomb, and how His body was laid". The women did not mistake the tomb!

On the morning of the first day of the week the women from Galilee (Luke 24:1-3) and Mary Magdalene and her Bethany friends (John 20:1,2), as they bring their spices to anoint the precious body, find the sealing-stone rolled away from the tomb the work of "an angel of the Lord descended from heaven" (Matthew 28:2-4). Some "entered in, and found not the body of the Lord Jesus" (Luke 24:1-3). Mary Magdalene rushed off to tell Peter and the other disciple, in these burning words, "They have taken away the Lord out of the tomb, and we know not where they have laid Him" (John 20:2).

Then followed the revelation from the "two men ... in dazzling apparel ... Why seek ye the living among the dead? He is not here, but is risen; remember how He spake unto you when He was yet in Galilee", saying that on the third day He would rise again (Luke 24:4-7). The declaration with regard to His resurrection according to Matthew (28:5-7) and Mark (16:5-7) gives more details' in that the young man arrayed in a white robe said, "Ye seek Jesus, the Nazarene, which hath been crucified: He is risen; He is not here: behold, the place where they laid Him! But go, tell His disciples and Peter". Sad, indeed, that these messages appeared in the sight of the apostles as idle talk; and they disbelieved them. But Peter and John were aroused, and they ran to investigate the "empty tomb" (Luke 24:12 and John 20:3-10). No one can read John's record of this visit without observing the striking marks of reality in the account. The position of the grave-clothes proves the impossibility of the theft of the body, either by friend or foe. A comparison of the description of the orderly arrangement of the winding linen cloths and the head-napkin in verses 6 and 7 with the incident recorded in John 11:44, when Lazarus left the tomb, is startling evidence that the Lord had risen and left the grave-clothes in perfect order.

The invented account of the disappearance of the body of the Lord, and the giving of bribes to the guards - a supposedly sleeping Roman guard - is not worth serious refutation. The Lord's disciples could not have moved the body in the face of the many hazards and obstacles, even were they brave enough at that period to have attempted it.

Within fifty days the apostles were boldly preaching the Resurrection of Jesus in the streets of Jerusalem. If then the Jews had taken the body from the tomb, why could they not produce the dead body and so silence forever the apostles' message? One has written "the silence of the Jews on this issue is as significant as the speech of the Christians". The only acceptable answer to the "empty tomb" is that the Lord Jesus was raised from the dead by the power of God, the Father, and that He left the tomb of His own volition, triumphant over the grave and sin and death, the Possessor of the keys of death and Hades! (Revelation 1:18).

There are two sets of appearances, one in Jerusalem and environs and the other in Galilee. Their weight of testimony as to the bodily resurrection of our blessed Lord is irrefutable. Luke, in his second treatise, records how the Lord "shewed Himself alive after His passion by many proofs" (Acts 1:2-3), appearing unto them (the apostles), whom He had chosen, by the space of forty days. Our Lord appeared to them where they were, wherever their fears or necessities had driven them; at the tomb, on the road to Emmaus, in the upper room, at locations known only to Himself (in the cases of Peter and James), by the sea of Tiberias, in Jerusalem, on a mountain slope in Galilee, and over against Bethany.

He first appeared by the empty tomb (Mark 16:9) to a single individual, Mary Magdalene, to one who loved Him much and who was richly rewarded for her long vigil in that lonely, sad burial-place. "Mary" and "Rabboni" are thrilling words in John's account of that first appearance of the risen Lord (John 20.11-18).

The number of witnesses who, together, beheld Him, varied; to two on a highway, to ten in the upper room, in Jerusalem, and a week later to the eleven as they sat at meat, to seven as they were fishing, and to five hundred in Galilee, and to one chosen servant on the Damascus highway. Some of these appearances are described by one or more of the Gospel writers. None of the Gospels claims to narrate every appearance of the Saviour to His disciples. The independence of these many manifestations and some dissimilarities in matters of detail but serve to corroborate the great central fact that the Lord had risen indeed.

STUDIES ON THE RESURRECTION OF CHRIST

It may be difficult to set each manifestation in its correct chronological place, but of the accumulative evidence of the Resurrection of our Lord and Saviour there remains not a vestige of doubt. The following tabular view of the manifestations of the Lord is submitted as a cumulative mass of unquestionable evidence.

Scripture references: Mark 16:9-11; John 20:11-18; Matthew 28:9-10; Mark 16:12,13; Luke 24:33,34; Mark 16:14; Luke 24:33,34; John 20:19-23; John 20:24-29; John 21:1-24; Matthew 28:16-20; Mark 16:15-18; Mark 16:19; Luke 24:50-53; Acts 1:69; 1 Corinthians 15:8

CHAPTER SIX: PIVOTAL IN THE APOSTLE'S PREACHING (JACK FERGUSON)

It is quite evident that the resurrection of the Lord Jesus featured much more prominently in the preaching of the apostles, and in the early years of the dispensation generally, than it does in our preaching today. This was doubtless due to the fact that the apostles were eye-witnesses of the miracle. It had transformed them. It had opened, as it were, the locked doors of the upper room in Jerusalem, and in the power of the newly given Spirit they had issued forth, we might almost say, "conquering, and to conquer". With the eleven came Matthias, the freshly chosen twelfth man, described by Peter as "a witness with us of His resurrection". This was the imperative feature of apostolic testimony, with what powerful and, indeed, infectious results we know.

To the early nucleus, in the language of the types, Benoni was now Benjamin. The Man of Calvary, crucified through weakness, was personally known to them to be living by the power of God, with the eternal glory, honour, and dominion. When, therefore, Paul, as one born out of due time, joined himself lifelong to the movement, his testimony was in perfect harmony with that of the pioneers of the Faith: "Have I not seen Jesus our Lord?" Jesus, as delivered up for their offences; our Lord, as raised again for their justification. Thus no one could condemn, since the living Lord was interceding. And from His love nothing could separate; no amount of "tribulation, or anguish, or persecution, or famine, or nakedness, or peril, or sword". So, taking their place in the age-long line of faithful witnesses to the things they had seen, heard, and most assuredly believed, they were joyfully prepared for His sake to be "killed all the day long ... accounted as sheep for the slaughter": killed, but more than conquerors. No wonder they were complete enigmas to their worldly contemporaries!

Interspersed throughout the book of Acts there are brief accounts of addresses given by the apostles and some powerful appeals by Paul. Acts 4:33 provides an excellent summary, "And with great power gave the apostles their witness of the resurrection of the Lord Jesus". They were fearless, irresistible heralds making proclamation on behalf of their absent King, as, for example, in Acts 2:36, "Let all the house of Israel therefore know assuredly, that God hath made Him both Lord and Christ, this Jesus whom ye crucified"; and again, in Acts 4:8-12, "Ye rulers of the people, and elders ... be it known unto you all, and to all the people of Israel, that in the name of Jesus Christ of Nazareth, whom ye crucified, whom God raised from the dead ... is there salvation. "Know assuredly" was the clarion, clear-cut call. There were no doubts or uncertainties about these preachers. They believed their beliefs. They had eaten and drunk with Him after His resurrection. They had seen the wound-prints, those engravings of which the prophet had spoken. Henceforth He was their absolute, living Lord and Master. And not only so, but He was also living in them. Therefore their determination, in a boldness which made even their adversaries to marvel, was that not only would He be preached by them but also that He would be revealed in them (Galatians 1:16), magnified (Philippians 1:20).

They were veritable balls of fire, these men, convinced about the brevity of time and the profound reality of eternity. Had they not heard from their Lord's own lips about eternal punishment and eternal life? Their battle-cry – "We cannot but speak the things which we saw and heard" (Acts 4:20). Their key words, "slew", "raised up", "witnesses". In due course one of the early band went from their midst the hard but glorious way. In his closing moments he saw clearly "the glory of God, and Jesus", and gave the martyr's testimony, "I see the heavens opened, and the Son of Man". Stephen died, stoned, but his power in testimony flowed on unabated in his fellows. Little wonder it is written, "So mightily grew the word of the Lord and prevailed." Great days, these!

To these men the resurrection of the Lord Jesus became a living, lively hope. They proclaimed "in Jesus the resurrection of the dead". His resurrection was the guarantee of their own-to eternal glory. Not only was He Lord of the living and the present, but to them He was also Lord of all, and of all time and eternity. Therefore they announced, "whom the heaven must receive until They saw clearly the coming day when He would restore all things. He would fill all the future with His glory. Bound up with this was the fact that He was also the God appointed Judge of the living and the dead. So they suitably warned the people with long and tender pleadings.

In every sense, their aim was to "know Him, and the power of His resurrection". With this went the fellowship of His sufferings and conformity to His death. That they would gladly accept. And beloved Paul doubtless spoke the feelings of them all when he said, "if by any means I may attain unto the resurrection from the dead", not the resurrection at the Rapture, for in that all believers would share, but a triumphant experience of out-resurrection here and now, a "present life of identification with Christ in resurrection" (Vine).

These then were the men whom the Lord used in building up the Church the Body, and in establishing the churches of God, in visible, corporate testimony, before the eyes of the nations. Single-minded men, their persuasions were to them deep convictions. They had no doubts nagging away at the back of their minds as to the reality of their Lord's own life in glory and His glorious dominance over theirs. Nor did they question for a moment the high calling of the spiritual movement which they helped forward on its outward thrust. They knew only too well, as skilled combatants, that doubts would only weaken the part they had to play, in serving for their own generation the counsel of God. Little wonder, then, words of the poet reach us today.

"Rise up, ye men of God, be done with lesser things", or, as the Spirit says, "Imitate their faith". There is a saying, "Believe your beliefs and doubt your doubts". There is a contrary tendency among some today to begin to believe their doubts and to doubt their beliefs. That will weaken the strongest. There are things, Luke says, "most surely believed among us" (Luke 1:1 KJV). They relate to the Faith, once for all delivered to the saints. It is one thing to look at these things with an inquiring mind so as to understand more perfectly the things we believe, but it is quite another and wrong to be for ever questioning, in the spirit of doubt and unbelief, to the undermining of our own faith and that of others. It looks as though the imminence of His coming means that we shall not have long to hold the precious truths committed to us. Till then, the Spirit says to the churches, "Look to yourselves that ye lose not the things which we have wrought, but that ye receive a full reward" (2 John 8).

CHAPTER SEVEN: PRESENT EFFECTS IN THE LIFE OF THE BELIEVER (JOHN DRAIN)

The resurrection of Christ gives us profound assurance that many things in the purposes of God have been fulfilled. It also guarantees the fulfilment of many things which await future developments of divine purpose. But there are also effects of the resurrection which should be felt in the present spiritual experience of believers in Christ.

Writing to persons who were knowing the strain and grief of persistent trials Peter said, "Blessed be the God and Father of our Lord Jesus Christ, who according to His great mercy begat us again unto a living hope by the resurrection of Jesus Christ from the dead, unto an inheritance ..." (1 Peter 1:3). Great and many are the blessings which come to the believing sinner when he is born again. Among these is the assured expectation of final deliverance from all trial and sorrow. The difficulties of the earthly pilgrimage will give place to the unspeakable glories of the eternal inheritance. The resurrection of Christ is the cause of this living hope being in our hearts and this hope imparts comfort and strength, lifting us above the depressing effects of trial, and directing us to the glorious day of the revelation of Jesus Christ. As the hymn-writer wrote: "Fair hope with what a sunshine does it cheer, Our roughest path on earth, our dreariest desert here."

In Romans 7:4, we read, "Wherefore, my brethren, ye also were made dead to the law through the body of Christ; that ye should be joined to Another, even to Him who was raised from the dead, that ye might bring forth fruit unto God". When we were in the flesh we brought forth fruit unto death (see Romans 6:21; 7:5). Our lives were not only God-dishonouring but also self-destroying. Sin brings wastage. In regeneration we were joined to the One who was raised from the dead so that by our union with this heavenly Man we should produce fruit which would give pleasure to God. This truth leads us to an examination of the doctrine of the Lord connected with baptism.

Paul having in Romans 5 shown the triumph of abounding grace immediately poses a probable rejoinder, "Shall we continue in sin, that grace may abound?" (Romans 6:1). In dealing with this matter the apostle demonstrates that persistence in sin though not a physical impossibility, is spiritually and logically unthinkable where there is a true understanding of the implications of baptism. When a person believes in Christ he enters into a new relationship with God. He is no longer in the flesh. He is in the Spirit and he is in Christ. In Christ he receives the free gift of God which is eternal life. Receiving the Person he receives the gift. Union with Christ means life, and the believer will for ever reign in life through Jesus Christ. But equally true is it that union with Christ means death for the believer.

Paul said, "I have been crucified with Christ" (Galatians 2:20). It is this important truth which is used by Paul when meeting the query. "Shall we continue in sin?" The believer's death with Christ has involved his death to sin. In baptism there is a physical showing forth of this reality. And Paul says, "We were buried therefore with Him through baptism into death: that like as Christ was raised from the dead through the glory of the Father, so we also might walk in newness of life". The resurrection of

Christ has a very important present message and meaning for His disciples. Those who died unto sin are to live unto God, unto Christ, "unto Him who for their sakes died and rose again" (2 Corinthians 5:15). We are linked with the resurrected Lord who is on the throne of God, and this association finds expression in a new kind of life, a life of resurrection power and character.

When writing his epistle to the Colossians Paul reminds those saints of things that had taken place in their spiritual experience. On the one hand they had been made perfect in Christ, "in Him ye are made full, who is the Head of all principality and power". On the other hand they had known a complete cutting off in the spiritual circumcision of Christ, and had been "buried with Him in baptism wherein ye were also raised with Him through faith in the working of God, who raised Him from the dead" (Colossians 2:12). One of the dangers affecting the saints in Colossae was a return to things to which they died. "If ye died with Christ from the rudiments of the world, why, as though living in the world, do ye subject yourselves to ordinances ...?" (Colossians 2:20).

This solemn challenge by the apostle was followed by the instructive exhortation, "If then ye were raised together with Christ, seek the things that are above, where Christ is, seated on the right hand of God. Set your mind on the things that are above, not on the things that are upon the earth". As believers in Christ we have, through amazing grace, been quickened together with Christ and raised up with Him and made to sit with Him in heavenly places. As His disciples we have been buried in baptism and raised to walk in newness of life. Perhaps there never was a time when there was such an abundance of things on this earth.

This constitutes a very grave danger for disciples of the Lord Jesus. There is so much to attract the mind and to grip the attention that we may become absorbed with the things upon the earth and lose sight of the things of highest value, the things that are above, the things of Jesus Christ. Home-life, education, employment, all have their legitimate place and claims in Christian life. The very important lesson to learn is what that place is. It is sad when it is true that we have, as the hymn-writer has said:

"Room for pleasure, room for business,

But for Christ the Crucified,

Not a place that He can enter,

In the heart for which He died".

To the godly women who came to the sepulchre on that memorable first day of the week the angel said, "He is not here; for He is risen". As we contemplate the world of men and women today and look upon the sin, corruption and lawlessness of this earthly scene perhaps we need to hear the voice that reminds us, "He is not here; for He is risen". The message of His resurrection should turn our thoughts to heaven and to heavenly things, and should raise us above the corrupting influences of earth to live in communion with the One who has been raised to the right hand of God.

The resurrection of Christ was a miracle of outstanding greatness and it demonstrated in a remarkable way the almighty power of God. The believer in Christ who desires to seek the things that are above, where Christ is, will need to experience the working of that same almighty power. Paul prayed for the saints in Ephesus that they might know "what (is) the exceeding greatness of His power to usward who believe, according to that working of the strength of His might which He wrought in Christ, when He raised Him from the dead ..." (Ephesians 1:19,20). It was such power that the apostle Paul wanted to know. He expressed the desire, "that I may know Him, and the power of His resurrection" (Philippians 3:16). If he would realize the spiritual experience of the fellowship of Christ's sufferings and conformity to His death, if he was to attain to the present enjoyment of a life of resurrection triumph in communion with the risen Christ, then he would need to know the power of Christ's resurrection.

This power is the actual divine power by which Christ was raised. It may also refer to the power that is felt in our lives through the assurance that Christ has been raised. When Paul was encouraging Timothy to take his part in suffering as a good soldier and servant of Christ Jesus he said, "Remember Jesus Christ, risen from the dead ..." There is stimulating power in such remembrance.

In 1 Corinthians 15 we have a profound and instructive examination of the subject of resurrection. In this examination, prominence is given to the resurrection of Christ, and the triumphant note is struck, "Now hath Christ been raised from the dead". The consequences of Christ's resurrection are many and far-reaching. In particular, the full weight of the assurance that the victorious Christ has been raised lies behind the exhortation, "Wherefore, my beloved brethren, be ye steadfast, unmoveable, always abounding in the work of the Lord, forasmuch as ye know that your labour is not vain in the Lord" (1 Corinthians 15:58).

CHAPTER EIGHT: PERPETUALLY HUMAN (JOHN TERRELL)

In His incarnation the Son of God became Man. Deity and humanity were both seen in reality and perfection in one Person for the first and only time in the history of the human race. In His humanity Christ was truly and fully man, body, soul, and spirit (see John 12:27, and Luke 23:46). Yet the wonder of His manhood finds its focus in His body of flesh and in the accomplishment therein of the work which the Father had given Him to do. In 1 Peter 2:24 we read "... who His own self bare our sins in His body upon the tree ..." Thus, in connection also with the Lord's resurrection, the central fact is that return to life of that same body which was tenderly and sorrowfully laid to rest in Joseph's sepulchre. So long as that wonderful body - called in Philippians 3:21 "the body of His glory" - is associated with the Lord no doubt can remain as to His continuing humanity.

We shall endeavour to show that the Lord's humanity was clearly preserved in resurrection; that it continues in heaven; and that it remains unchanged in connection with His coming again and our enjoyment with Him of the glorious eternal state. In doing so we shall consider initially a few scriptures bearing on the subject generally; then examine certain of the titles and offices of the Lord which in Scripture are clearly inseparable from His perpetual humanity; and finally we shall review the relationship of this great truth to the believer's hope of resurrection and eternal joy in the Master's presence.

There is no doubt from the record of Scripture that in resurrection the Lord was to all ordinary appearances a man. Mary mistakenly identified Him with the gardener (John 20:15). The two disciples journeying to Emmaus accepted their Fellow Traveller as such and offered Him hospitality. It was only after the Lord was recognized that the stupendous wonder of the situation created doubt as to its reality in the minds of the disciples in the closed room in Jerusalem. Those who saw Him without recognition saw simply a man who looked like other men. These facts themselves are surely eloquent testimony and indicate clearly that it was the Lord's intention that He should be accepted as the same Man who had yielded His life on the cross.

Yet in His deep understanding of the disciples' reaction to His appearing in resurrection He went to great lengths to reassure them of His humanity. Luke 24:39 may almost be viewed as settling the entire question of the Lord's humanity in resurrection. "See My hands and My feet, that it is I Myself; handle Me, and see; for a spirit hath not flesh and bones, as ye behold Me having". In John 4:24 we have the Master's own words, "God is a spirit", whereas in resurrection He says, "a spirit hath not flesh and bones, as ye behold Me having". No contradiction is seen here. On the contrary, surely the Lord was underlining with complete finality that in resurrection He remained Man as well as God. When the same precious and wounded hands were held out to Thomas, his earnest profession was, "My Lord and my God". At the time of the Lord's ascension there is great force and significance in the assurance of the angels, "This Jesus ... shall so come in like manner". He had shown Himself alive, after His passion, by many proofs. It was this Jesus who would return, this

Man of flesh and bones, this Man of the torn brow, of the pierced hands and feet, and of the wounded side.

We read in Colossians 2:9, "In Him dwelleth all the fulness of the Godhead bodily". Relating this tremendous statement to the unique exposition of the Person of Christ in Colossians 1, "Firstborn of all creation" (v.15); "Firstborn from the dead" (v.18), we recognize the divine seal to the truth of the uninterrupted humanity of the Lord Jesus as He is in heaven today. The Son of God was manifested bodily on earth at His incarnation; He is manifested bodily in heaven today, His perfect humanity still associated with the fulness of deity.

Pursuing the subject now to consider the Lord's humanity in relation to some of His offices and titles, we would turn attention to 1 Corinthians 15:45-49. Here the Lord Jesus is referred to as "the last Adam". The first Adam was the head of a race of living beings - "first that which is natural". The last Adam is the Head and Leader of a race of transformed, redeemed human beings who have been given spiritual life by Him – "then that which is spiritual". But they remain human beings, and their glorious Leader and Life-giver is a Man, as indeed the name Adam indicates. Similarly, in Romans 5:11-19, we have the spiritual correspondence of the Lord to Adam clearly shown; and the many who were made sinners set over against the many made righteous.

Another aspect of this truth is seen in connection with the Lord's Headship of the Church which is His Body. The redeemed human beings who compose this glorious thing, "My Church" (Matthew 16:18), have as their Head the Christ of resurrection supremacy (Ephesians 1:20-23). The members are to "grow up in all things into Him which is the Head, even Christ" (Ephesians 4:15). It will be clear that the humanity of the Lord Jesus is essential to the unity of Head and members in one organic whole (Colossians 2:19), although the matter of the physical body of the Lord, or of the members, is not prominent here. The glorified manhood of Christ is essential in this great mystery "which in other generations was not made known unto the sons of men" (Ephesians 3:4,5).

In 1 Timothy 2:5 we read a fundamental truth: "For there is one God, one Mediator also between God and men, Himself Man, Christ Jesus". These words are written by Paul in the context of the divine will that all men should be saved and come to the knowledge of the truth. The Lord's work as Mediator is integral here with His humanity. Does not this cast our minds back to the vivid Old Testament type in the book of Ruth of the near kinsman redeemer? Today mediation between God and men can only be effected through that same blessed Man, that matchless Mediator in the glory. Men of all races are daily being drawn to God by "the cords of a Man" (Hosea 11:4). Glorious truth indeed concerning the ministry of the heavenly Man, "this same Jesus"! We can with profit follow the truth of Christ, raised and in heaven, as the Mediator of a new covenant (Hebrews 8:6; 9:15; 12:24).

In the last of these references in Hebrews it is finally to "Jesus the Mediator of a new covenant" that we are come in the heavenly Zion. But inseparable from the truth of Christ as the Mediator between God and men is the solemn truth of His appointed office as Judge of the world. In Acts 17 we have the fascinating account of Paul's visit to Athens. The great preacher of Jesus and the resurrection thrusts home His Mars Hill message with the words, "Now He commandeth men that they should all everywhere repent: inasmuch as He hath appointed a day, in the which He will judge the world in righteousness by the Man whom He hath ordained; whereof He hath given assurance unto all men, in that He hath raised Him from the dead". Could the Holy Spirit make it clearer that the Judge of men is none else than the Man whose resurrection gives assurance of this truth?

Finally, in examining some of the risen Lord's exalted offices, let us look at our great High Priest. In this gracious capacity the lasting humanity of the Lord Jesus is seen by the believer perhaps more preciously than anywhere else. Once again the epistle to the Hebrews is our mine of spiritual treasure. Firstly we have His patient and all-understanding work for the people of God.

We draw attention to Hebrews 2:17 and 4:1-16. The former verse shows clearly that the Lord Jesus became truly a Man – "in all things to be made like unto His brethren" - not only to redeem men, but also to serve them in the heavens as "a merciful and faithful High Priest in things pertaining to God". Does not this mighty revelation give a wondrous depth and add new glorious dimensions to the truth of the incarnation of the Son of God and His continuing humanity? For this loving service to those whom He is not ashamed to call His brethren is given its deep and penetrating sympathy and compassion by His very humanity. The heart of every believer warms and thrills to the truth of Hebrews 4:15, the eternal God of creation glory, in His perfect humanity "touched with the feeling of our infirmities". The tireless feet that stood by a sepulchre outside Bethany, the beautiful hands that touched the bier by the gate of Nain, the eyes of yearning pity that wept over Jerusalem, are now daily employed in resurrection glory on behalf of us, flesh-encumbered men on earth.

Then with regard to the approach of the people of God into the Holies, we see in Hebrews 10:19,20 the association of "His flesh" with our access there. At least one translator speaks here of His flesh as His "human nature". What a boldness of confidence it gives to a holy priesthood to recognize the perfect and sinless humanity of the Great Priest over the house of God, and to avail ourselves with deep thankfulness of that "new and living way"!

And so we pass on to the third aspect of our study of the Lord's perpetual humanity-the believer's resurrection hope of sharing His likeness. "We know that, if He shall be manifested, we shall be like Him; for we shall see Him even as He is". In these words John the apostle writes with complete confidence to beloved saints of God. Now it will be evident, we suggest, that the humanity of Redeemer and redeemed are seen in the likeness of Christ which the believer is to share. Paul takes this truth right into the physical realm in Philippians 3:21, "who shall fashion anew the body of our humiliation, that it may be conformed to the body of His glory".

Our eternal humanity in glorified state is unmistakably identified with His. No question arises of deity for men. We shall enjoy in eternity redeemed and glorified humanity. We are "foreordained to be conformed to the image of His Son, that He might be the Firstborn among many brethren" (Romans 8:29). "And", says the apostle, as he prepares to wind up his masterly treatise on resurrection in 1 Corinthians 15, "as we have borne the image of the earthy, we shall also bear the image of the heavenly". Changed in the twinkling of an eye; corruption puts on incorruption; mortal puts on immortality, and death is swallowed up in victory.

Thus in the eternal counsels of Deity, we see the believer as "foreordained to be conformed to the image of His Son"; as to his present experience rejoicing daily with deep thankfulness for the heavenly Man who is our High Priest before the face of God; and anticipating his promised refashioning into his glorious Master's likeness. With all this convergence of truth concerning our Lord's unending humanity, and especially as we contemplate with John the apostle the eternal satisfaction of awaking in His likeness, we are left very directly challenged to sanctification by John's following word, "Every one that hath this hope set on him purifieth himself, even as He is pure" (1 John 3:3).

CHAPTER NINE: POST-RESURRECTION ASCENDER (P.W. ATKINSON)

Our thoughts at the outset go to a sorrowing woman standing beside an empty tomb. Mary Magdalene weeps for her Lord, whose body she supposes has been taken away, for as yet she knew not that He had risen. As she hears the voice she does not realize who it is that speaks, until He calls, "Mary"! The truth dawns upon her sorrowing mind and, with joy, she cries out, "Rabboni"! We note carefully His words, "Touch Me not; for I am not yet ascended unto the Father" (John 20:17). We pause and marvel at the grace of our Lord Jesus Christ, in appearing to Mary and comforting her troubled heart, before He ascended unto the Father.

Shortly after this meeting, the Lord Jesus Christ meets a group of women and as they hear His words, "All hail", it is recorded that they "came and took hold of His feet, and worshipped Him" (Matthew 28:9). Why was it that Mary was forbidden to touch Him, whereas, later, others were allowed to clasp His feet? The inference is that between these two meetings, the Lord Jesus had ascended unto the Father and presented Himself in fulfilment of the Old Testament type of the waving of the sheaf of the firstfruits on the morrow after the sabbath (Leviticus 23:11) i.e. the first day of the week - the resurrection morn. He is "the firstfruits of them that are asleep" (1 Corinthians 15:20) and as such, we suggest, He entered heaven above to stand before the Father as the Victor over death and Hell.

However, there was work on earth yet to be done before He could sit down on the right hand of the Majesty on high. His loved disciples needed preparation for the work of establishing the kingdom of God and had much to learn which they were not ready to receive before His death and resurrection. So, during forty days, the risen Lord appears to the apostles speaking the things concerning the kingdom of God (Acts 1:3), firmly implanting into their minds and hearts the principles which would be passed on to others by them. On the fortieth day, having now completed His talks with the apostles, He raises His hands and blesses them (Luke 24:50). Then, as they stand amazed, He rises from, the ground and commences to ascend into heaven. Their eyes follow Him upward until a cloud receives Him out of their sight, "and He "was received up into heaven, and sat down at the right hand of God" (Mark 16:19).

From the foregoing, we have suggested that there was (a) the ascension between His revealing Himself to Mary alone, and the later meeting with the women, and (b) the ascension forty days after, when He took His seat on high after completing His ministry to the apostles. Thus His ascension was twofold-firstly, private and unseen to mortal eye, later witnessed by the apostles. Perhaps the Spirit of God by the Psalmist gave a hint of this, in the repetition of the words, "Lift up your heads, O ye gates; and be ye lift up, ye everlasting doors; and the King of Glory shall come in" (Psalm 24:7-8). His entrance into heaven was majestic, and He is lauded as "the LORD strong and mighty". Truly, the triumphant entry of the Victor!

Nor did He enter alone, for there were the spoils which He had won in His victory. "Wherefore He saith, 'When He ascended on high, He led captivity captive ... "(Ephesians 4:8) He wrested from the devil the keys of death and Hades (Revelation 1:18). "When the strong man fully armed guardeth his own court, his goods are in peace: but when a stronger than he shall come upon him, and overcome him, he taketh from him his whole armour wherein he trusted, and divideth his spoils" (Luke 11:21,22). Rising from among the dead, the glorious Victor led forth from Satan's domain a multitude of captives - the Old Testament saints whose souls had been waiting in upper Sheol - to accompany Him in His triumphant entry into the glory.

Let us now consider what it meant to the Son of God again to take His place at the right hand of God. When on earth He had the knowledge that "He came forth from God, and goeth unto God" (John 13:3), and just prior to the cross, He lifted up His eyes into heaven and prayed, "And now, O Father, glorify Thou Me with the glory which I had with Thee before the world was," (John 17:5). When He came into the world on the work of redemption, He "emptied Himself, taking the form of a servant ... " (Philippians 2:7), but, when the work was finished and He had risen from the dead, then He would return to God to know the blessedness of His glorification by the Father and to take His seat beside Him. This position was His from all past eternity, but for a little while, He had descended to earth and into the grave, in order to effect our redemption. The work now completed, He has the boundless joy of again entering into His glory (Luke 24:26).

Long centuries before, the Psalmist had recorded the words of Messiah's expectation, "Thou wilt show Me the path of life: in Thy presence is fulness of joy; in Thy right hand there are pleasures for evermore" (Psalm 16:11). The apostle Peter, by the Holy Spirit, takes up this prophetic word in his message to Israel concerning the Lord Jesus Christ on the day of Pentecost. He speaks of the resurrection: "Thou madest known unto Me the ways of life; Thou shalt make Me full of gladness with Thy countenance" (Acts 2:28). The personal joy and gladness of the Lord Jesus as He entered again into the glory above as the victorious One, is indescribable. Our finite minds cannot grasp the overflowing greatness of His pleasure. Just as His sorrow on earth and on the Cross was beyond the understanding of man "Behold, and see if there be any sorrow like unto My sorrow" (Lamentations 1:12), so His joy and gladness in His ascension are outside the range of our capabilities to enter into in any measure.

The prophetic words of the Psalmist are also taken up by the writer of the epistle to the Hebrews, concerning the Son of God, "Thou hast loved righteousness and hated iniquity; therefore God, Thy God, bath anointed Thee with the oil of gladness above Thy fellows" (Hebrews 1:9). Yes, as we meditate upon His deep sorrow, His pain and agony, how it lifts our hearts and brings forth praise and worship, when we remember that His "sorrows all are o'er" He suffered "once for all" and never again will He have to endure as He did, and now, He has joy, gladness and pleasure above all others beside.

The lofty tones of Hebrews 1 ring out, "Who being the effulgence of His glory, and the very image of His substance, and upholding all things by the word of His power, when He had made purification of sins, sat down on the right hand of the Majesty on high; having become by so much better than the angels, as He hath inherited a more excellent name than they".

CHAPTER TEN: PERFECT BODY (LAURIE BURROWS)

"He that was dead came forth, bound hand and foot with grave clothes; and his face was bound about with a napkin" (John 11:44). These strange words were not spoken of the Lord but of Lazarus of Bethany, whose experience carries instruction for us by way of contrast with the circumstances of the Lord's resurrection. Lazarus could not resume the ordinary routine of life until the grave clothes had been removed by his friends. Scripture thus emphasizes the mortal limitations that still affected him, in spite of the unprecedented demonstration of divine power in the raising to life of a man who had been dead four days. The Lord's resurrection must have been quite different in character, for He left His grave clothes behind in the tomb (Luke 24:12; John 20:1-10). Who removed them? Was it His Father or an angel, or the Lord Himself?

In the empty tomb on that eventful resurrection morning there seems to have been something striking about the disposition of the grave-clothes which perplexed Peter and John. If they had been unwound and left lying in the tomb, some straightforward explanation would undoubtedly have suggested itself, but what John saw caused him to look more closely, with the result that he believed (John 20:8), and Peter wondered "at that which was come to pass" (Luke 24:12). If the Lord's body in the act of resurrection passed through the grave-clothes, leaving them undisturbed, it would have been immediately appreciated by any observant visitor to the empty tomb that a great miracle had taken place. The actions of Peter and John would thus be adequately explained (John 20:1-10).

They abandoned their investigation and returned thoughtfully home, convinced that Mary Magdalene was mistaken in her original assumption that the Lord's body had been stolen. The suggested manner of the Lord's resurrection is also in complete harmony with the miraculous manner of some of His appearances to the disciples. On two occasions He suddenly appeared in the room with them although the doors were securely closed (John 20:9,26). At another time he vanished after eating a meal with two disciples in their home at Emmaus (Luke 24:31).

In order to obtain a balanced view of the matter and avoid the implication that the Lord's resurrection body was in some way insubstantial, other scriptures should be examined. Matthew 28:9 describes how that soon after His resurrection He appeared to certain women who took hold of His feet in an act of worship. He invited unbelieving Thomas to touch His hands and side, where the marks of Calvary still remained, but the sight alone was sufficient to renew Thomas's faith (John 20:26-29).

The Lord gave a similar invitation to the disciples on the resurrection day, but their first reaction was terror, imagining that they were in the presence of a spirit. This mistake was due to His sudden and mysterious appearance among them, when His tragic death was still vivid in their memories. It was not due to his outward appearance, which could not have been spirit-like, for the Lord Himself said, "A spirit hath not flesh and bones, as ye behold Me having" (Luke 24:39). It is clear from this statement that the Lord's resurrection body was a human structure of bones covered with flesh; it was unnecessary for the Lord to include any reference to His blood in His description of what could be seen outwardly and we suggest that no inference as to lack of blood in the Lord's body can be drawn from the omission. He said to the disciples, "It is I Myself", an absolute confirmation that the same Person whom they followed for three years was again with, them in resurrection life. His flesh did not see corruption (Acts 2:31).

It is not possible for us with our present knowledge to understand how the Lord in resurrection could company with the disciples, eat and drink with them and discourse with them, displaying all the traits of a true Man and yet be able to appear and disappear at will (Acts 10:40-42). Some help may be obtained from Philippians 3:21, where the refashioning of the believer's body at the coming of the Lord is referred to as resulting in a body like the body of His glory.

This aspect of resurrection will be dealt with more fully in another chapter in this book, but we mention the scripture because it confirms that the Lord has a body today, but it is a "body of glory". In its context the phrase implies that the Lord on earth had a body of humiliation subject to restrictions of locality and time and the necessity to eat and sleep. These limitations were then in a sense necessary, being suspended only on a few exceptional occasions, but now they have been removed for ever, although they were resumed voluntarily for short periods for the purpose of communicating with the disciples during the forty days following the resurrection.

It may be contended that the difficulty which was at times experienced by the disciples in recognizing the Lord after the resurrection points to a more far-reaching change than we have suggested. For instance, on the resurrection day the two travellers to Emmaus conversed with him for at least two hours, not realizing His identity. Mary Magdalene was slow in recognizing Him, and the disciples fishing on Lake Tiberius had changed their nets from one side of the boat to the other and were struggling with a large catch before they were convinced that the Stranger whose advice they had taken was indeed the Lord. Some of these instances could be accounted for by the fact that the trials of the Lord's earthly life were over; no longer was He the weary persecuted Man of Sorrows, He was the glorified triumphant Lord. Such a vast change must have been reflected in His appearance.

Another likely explanation is that on some occasions it suited the Lord's immediate purpose to remain incognito for a time. When conversing with Cleopas and his friend (Luke 24:13-35) it was essential that they should listen carefully as He explained the detailed fulfilment of Messianic prophecy in the Old Testament, an object which would not have been achieved had they been excited on meeting the Lord for the first time after His resurrection. So the eyes of the disciples were not at first allowed to recognize Him (Luke 24:16), but Mark 16:12 may indicate that there was also some change in the Lord.

Joy and wonder overcame the disciples when they saw the Lord in His resurrection body; the memory of that sight and of the wounds sustained on their account were a powerful influence in their lives, given in service to Him. But disciples in this present day who believe by the exercise of faith rather than by the sight of the eyes are assured of a special blessing (John 20:29), and we can look forward to the day when we shall see Him even as He is. Then He will say to us as He said to the apostles, "See My hands and My feet, that it is I Myself" (Luke 24:39); our Saviour and Lord!

CHAPTER ELEVEN: PROVEN BY THE EVIDENCE (DAVID HYLAND)

That Jesus Christ lived and died is widely accepted. Many claim that they find the evidence for the resurrection of Christ less reliable historically than that for His death. From the time of the event to the present day, the truth of the resurrection has been challenged from several points of view. If the doubts cast on the truth of the Biblical account of the resurrection could be shown to have any substance, this would seriously impair the reliability of the Christian gospel. The challenge of the sceptics cannot be ignored.

The resurrection of Christ is a major truth of the Christian faith. Paul, recounting the essential facts of the gospel he received by revelation from God writes, "Christ died for our sins ... was buried ... and hath been raised" (1 Corinthians 15:3,4). He then states, "If Christ hath not been raised, then is our preaching vain, your faith also is vain. Yea, and we are found false witnesses of God; because we witnessed of God that He raised up Christ ... If Christ hath not been raised, your faith is vain; ye are yet in your sins" (1 Corinthians 15:14-17). This is a forceful statement of the issues involved. If Christ is not alive, believers have been completely misled and are to be pitied.

It is significant that when the Lord was challenged to indicate a sign to place His authority and teaching beyond question, He referred to His approaching death and resurrection, 'Destroy this temple, and in three days I will raise it up" (John 2:19). The Jews completely misunderstood what the Lord said; they assumed He referred to the temple in Jerusalem. The disciples had limited understanding at the time the statement was made. After the resurrection, the recollection of the Lord's words strengthened their faith. They then realized that "He spake of the temple of His body" (John 2:21). All that the Lord had claimed about His Person, His works and His teaching is vindicated by His resurrection. The mind that accepts the truth of the resurrection of Christ will not boggle at any of the other miracles.

To establish the truth of the resurrection of Christ it is first necessary to find sufficient evidence for the reality of His death. The Roman soldiers were competent executioners. Their lives could be in jeopardy if they failed to secure the death of a sentenced prisoner. The centurion who was commanding officer at the crucifixion was able to certify the death to Pilate. To make absolutely sure, one of the soldiers pierced the Lord's side with a spear. John records that "blood and water" flowed from this wound, proof that the Man on the middle cross was dead. Nevertheless, some have denied that the Lord actually died. It is suggested that He fainted, or fell into a coma through loss of blood. Then, it is claimed, the chill of the tomb and the aroma of the spices combined to revive Him; and, leaving the tomb, He made Himself known to His disciples. But the evidence is strongly against the theory of a swoon. This attempt to explain the resurrection appearances ignores the events which led up to the Lord's burial. Pilate was convinced that the Lord was dead before giving Joseph of Arimathea permission to remove the body from the cross. It was because the Lord was already dead that the soldier did not break His legs. Instead he' pierced His side.

The earliest attempt to explain the empty tomb was to suggest that the body had been stolen. When the guards reported to the chief priests that the tomb was empty, they were bribed to say, "His disciples came by night, and stole Him away while we slept" (Matthew 28:13). The guards put this story about, and it persisted at the time Matthew wrote his Gospel. When guards are set, some watch while others sleep. It is unlikely that the whole guard would sleep through the removing of the stone. Sleeping men cannot possibly say what happened. If all the guards admit to being asleep, and then all tell the same story, this would be clear evidence of collusion.

The truth of the resurrection of Christ formed an important part of the message of His disciples. If they had anything to do with the removal of the body, they could not have preached with conviction. They not only preached what they believed - they suffered for it. The disciples were prepared to go to prison for the truth they taught. It is inconceivable that they would be prepared to do this knowing that the message they preached was based on a fabrication. What explains the transformation of the disciples from fearful men who met behind closed doors for fear of the Jews into fearless heralds of the gospel who went out and preached boldly? The transformation can only be understood in the light of the resurrection appearances of their Master, who charged them to carry out the great commission and sent the Holy Spirit to empower them to do it.

Of all the theories of theft, the suggestion that the Jewish authorities were responsible for secretly removing the body is the most unlikely. If the leaders of the Jews had the body, they would have produced the one piece of evidence which would have destroyed the credibility of the disciples. By hiding the body they would have helped the spread of the teaching they wished to suppress.

Some sceptics have described Mary Magdalene as the weak link in the chain of testimony to the truth of the resurrection. Those who question the reliability of Mary as a witness of the resurrection express doubts as to whether she was healed of her demon-possession by the Lord. It is then claimed that owing to mental or emotional instability Mary was subject to hallucinations. The loss of her Friend, Jesus of Nazareth, they say, had induced in her a state of hysteria and heightened her powers of imagination. The wish was father to the thought; she imagined she saw the Lord. Then, it is supposed, Mary persuaded others, or others persuaded themselves that they also had seen Him.

But the Lord also appeared to the disciples. Were they all subject to the same delusion? On one occasion the Lord appeared to above five hundred brethren at once" (1 Corinthians 15:6). It is impossible that all this company should experience a similar delusion at the same time. Hallucinations are intensely personal, arising in the subconscious mind of the individual. No two persons will experience exactly the same delusion. Hallucinations relate to the hopes or fears that occupy the mind. But all the evidence suggests that the disciples were not expecting these appearances of the Lord. As the two who were travelling to Emmaus said, "We hoped that it was He which should redeem Israel" (Luke 24:21). When the Lord did reveal Himself to His disciples they were surprised.

Some of the carping objections that have been raised to challenge the truth of the resurrection have been briefly examined.

The conclusion is inevitable that the evidence for the resurrection is incontrovertible and the witnesses are unimpeachable. The Gospels have the ring of truth; the resurrection is an historical fact. But the significance of the resurrection is not limited to its historicity. The resurrection is God's seal of approval upon the atoning death of His Son. It signifies that God's just requirements have been met. Because of the death and resurrection of Christ, His righteousness can be imputed to the believing sinner. The Lord Jesus Christ was delivered up for our trespasses, and was raised for our justification" (Romans 4:25).

The apostle Paul was very aware of the historical significance of the resurrection of Christ. He also stressed its doctrinal significance as a major truth of the Faith. Moreover Paul had an intense personal longing that the resurrection life of Christ might have an impact on his own personal life. "That I may know Him, and the power of His resurrection" (Philippians 3:10). If we share Paul's longing it will be to the glory of God and the blessing of others.

CHAPTER TWELVE: PROMISED RETURN (ALAN TOMS)

The land from which I write is one shrouded in darkness and the shadow of death. "Having no hope and without God in the world" is an apt description of so many of its people. Why is it so? One main reason is because they follow leaders who are dead. Against such a sombre background the hope of the Christian shines so brightly, for we serve a living Saviour. "Why seek ye the living among the dead?" questioned the angels on that most glorious first day of the week, "He is not here, but is risen" Therein lies the believer's hope. It springs from an empty tomb and is centred in a risen Lord.

The bodily resurrection of the Lord Jesus lies at the foundation of our faith, for "if Christ hath not been raised, your faith is vain; ye are yet in your sins" (1 Corinthians 15:17). "But now hath Christ been raised from the dead" (verse 20). Oh, the glorious certainty of it! This fact flooded the lives of the early Christians, giving them new purpose and hope and empowering all their service. They lived in the expectation of the return of their risen Lord.

Recalling his work among the Thessalonians, Paul wrote to them, "ye turned unto God from idols, to serve a living and true God, and to wait for His Son from heaven, whom He raised from the dead, even Jesus" (I Thessalonians 1:9,10). They turned, to serve and to wait, and their waiting was no vain hope. The empty tomb was their assurance that He would return. And so it is still. We have been begotten again "unto a living hope by the resurrection of Jesus Christ from the dead" (1 Peter 1:3). Hope looks back to an empty tomb, upward to an occupied throne, and onward to the return in glorified body of the Man who sits upon it.

"We hoped that it was He which should redeem Israel", said the two disconsolate disciples as they communed with the Stranger on the Emmaus road. But when their eyes were opened and they knew Him, hope blazed afresh and they returned that very night to Jerusalem with their glad message, "The Lord is risen indeed".

THE PROMISE OF HIS RETURN

"Where is the promise of His coming?" cry the mockers of whom Peter warned us. There is no lack of such people today, who treat the word of God as a plaything, for that is the thought behind the word "mockers". But the taunts of the unbelieving only serve to strengthen the believer's faith.

"If I go … I come again, and will receive you unto Myself", said the Master Himself. And He did go, for "as they were looking, He was taken up; and a cloud received Him out of their sight" (Acts 1:9). So surely will He return. "This Jesus, which was received up from you into heaven, shall so come in like manner as ye beheld Him going into heaven", said the angels to those wondering disciples. And to the testimony of the Lord Jesus and the angels is added that of the apostles. "The Lord Himself shall descend from heaven, with a shout, with the voice of the archangel, and with the trump of God" (1 Thessalonians 4:16). Could words be plainer? They leave no room for doubt. "A threefold cord is not quickly broken". "He that cometh shall

STUDIES ON THE RESURRECTION OF CHRIST 67

come, and shall not tarry" (Hebrews 10:37). In happy confidence we rest upon His word, "looking for the blessed hope and appearing of the glory of our great God and Saviour Jesus Christ" (Titus 2:13).

THE MANNER OF HIS RETURN

Four interesting Greek words are used by the Spirit of God to describe the Lord's return.

(a) His presence (parousia) is the most common. It denotes not only the arrival of a person but also his continuing presence. Paul uses the word in Philippians 2.12 of his presence among the saints, in contrast to his absence from them. Our Master is absent now as to His bodily presence. He has gone away, and our hearts warm at the prospect of His soon coming again. His parousia includes His coming to the air for His saints, and His presence with them from that moment to the time when He returns with all His saints to commence His reign on earth.

(b) Another word used, particularly by Peter, is apokalupsis, translated "at the revelation of Jesus Christ" (1 Peter 1:7,13). It is used both in connection with His coming to the air and His coming in judgement to the earth (2 Thessalonians 1:7). It means "to uncover" (apo, from, and kalupto, to cover). "At the revelation of His glory also ye may rejoice with exceeding joy" (1 Peter 4:13). Then He will be unveiled and we shall see Him, whom not having seen, we love, and our wondering hearts will exclaim, "I had heard of Thee by the hearing of the ear: but now mine eye seeth Thee" (Job 42:5).

"Our Lord's coming draweth nigh,

His long-sought unveiling:

Let us Maranatha cry

With a faith unfailing."

(c) The third word, epiphaneia, is literally "a shining forth". It is used of His first coming in grace, when the Word became flesh and dwelt among us, and also of His second coming, both for His saints to the air and with His saints to the earth. "That thou keep the commandment, without spot, without reproach, until the appearing of our Lord Jesus Christ" (1 Timothy 6:14). What a shining forth that will be!

(d) A fourth word, very similar to the above (for it comes from the same root, phan, shining) is phaneroo, to be manifested, to make visible. "And when the Chief Shepherd shall be manifested, ye shall receive the crown of glory that fadeth not away" (1 Peter 5:4).

All four words are required to describe the glory of that wonderful moment when at His presence He will be unveiled to our sight, manifested firstly to His own and then to the world and His glory will shine forth. Christian, what a time that will be! Blessed hope indeed! Are we living in the expectation of it?

"Are we watching for the Master?

For His coming draweth near:

Are we ready for the moment,

When He shall for us appear?"

THE INDICATIONS OF HIS RETURN

"Tell us, when shall these things be?" asked the disciples, and although they did not receive a direct answer to their question, for times or seasons the Father hath set within His own authority, yet in the teaching which their question drew forth the Lord Jesus foretold many events which would indicate the nearness of His return as Son of Man. We are living in momentous days when some of these things are beginning to take shape. "Ye shall hear of wars and rumours of wars ... nation shall rise against nation, and kingdom against kingdom" (Matthew 24:6,7). This is becoming increasingly true, isn't it?

"There shall be famines and earthquakes in diverse places" (verse 7). It is said that starvation kills more than four million people in a year and that 70% of children under the age of six suffer from malnutrition. Within recent memory, great earthquakes have claimed many lives in countries both East and West. "In diverse places famines and pestilences" (Luke 21:11). Deadly diseases are on the increase despite the rapid progress of medical science. "Iniquity shall be multiplied" (Matthew 24:12). Constant lowering of moral standards is turning the world into a cesspool of iniquity. "Evil men and impostors shall wax worse and worse" (2 Timothy 3:13).

Drug-peddlers are after our young people in schools and colleges, eager to blight any young lives that come within their grasp. Impurity is openly paraded and pictures of a seductive nature are screened for all to see at the turn of the television switch. "Men fainting for fear, and for expectation of the things which are coming on the world" (Luke 21:26). The nations continue their wild atomic race, piling up weapons of destruction sufficient to blast millions into eternity. The thoughtful man trembles if he does not know the Lord. As for the pleasure-seeking multitude, "eat, drink and be merry" is their philosophy of life as Satan successfully fascinates their minds with the passing things of time. But perhaps that which speaks most loudly of all to those who love the Scriptures is the little nation of Israel, set in its strategic central position both in the world and in the purposes of God. "From the fig tree learn her parable: when her branch is now become tender, and putteth forth its leaves, ye know that the summer is nigh; even so ye also, when ye see these things coming to pass, know ye that He is nigh, even at the doors" (Mark 13:28,29).

THE CHALLENGE OF HIS RETURN

The believer cannot and dare not close his eyes to these plain indications of the Master's soon return. How will He find us when He comes? At ease in Zion? Or pressing on toward the goal? With our pounds and talents buried or diligently trading therewith until He come? If we have been sleeping, it is high time for us to awake out of sleep; for now is salvation nearer to us than when we first believed. The night is far spent and the day is at hand. Our risen Lord sits on high, "from henceforth expecting ..." This is our opportunity to offer ourselves willingly in the day of His power. "What is our hope, or joy, or crown of glorying?" Happy shall we be if, like the apostle, we can point to some and say, "Are not even ye, before our Lord Jesus at His coming?" (1 Thessalonians 2:19).

"Can we, dare we disappoint Him?

Brethren, let us rise.

He who died for us is calling

From the skies."

CHAPTER THIRTEEN: PREFIGURING OUR RESURRECTION (FRED EVANS)

The resurrection of the dead was the hope of the great men of God in Old Testament times. This is clear from many Scriptures but two clear examples should suffice to illustrate the point. The language of Job is explicit: "I know that my Redeemer liveth, and that He shall stand up at the last upon the earth: and after my skin hath been thus destroyed, yet from my flesh shall I see God: whom I shall see for myself, and mine eyes shall behold, and not another" (Job 19:25-27). Speaking with certainty, he looked forward to seeing his Redeemer standing on the earth in the future (at the last). It would almost seem as if he had an understanding not only of his own resurrection but also of the incarnation of the Son of God, when he said, "From my flesh shall I see God".

Whereas Job spoke of his own personal future, Daniel made a collective and general statement, involving the resurrection of many, the just and the unjust, "Many of them that sleep in the dust of the earth shall awake, some to everlasting life, and some to shame and everlasting contempt. And they that be wise shall shine as the brightness of the firmament; and they that turn many to righteousness as the stars for ever and ever" (Daniel 12:2,3).

It is not surprising that the Lord Jesus Christ condemned the Sadducees, who denied the resurrection, because they knew not the Scriptures, nor the power of God. The Old Testament does not only teach the resurrection of the dead, but as if to give illustration of God's power over death, there are three cases of dead ones being raised. The son of the widow of Zarephath was raised to life when Elijah called upon God in prayer and "the soul of the child came into him again". The great woman of Shunem's son was raised when Elisha, having "shut the door upon them twain, and prayed unto the LORD", stretched himself upon the child seven times, and the child opened his eyes. Also when an unknown man was being hurriedly buried in time of invasion, his body was cast into the sepulchre of Elisha, and as soon as it touched the bones of the dead prophet, he revived and stood up on his feet.

Similar illustrations are given during the lifetime of the Lord, when He demonstrated His power by raising individual persons who had died. If we include the raising of the daughter of Jairus, the number is again three. The daughter was raised while she was in the house, obviously shortly after death. The only son of the widow of Nain was brought to life in the street, while he lay on the bier in the funeral procession. Lazarus of Bethany was restored to life from the grave, four days after his death. Different circumstances, different ages, different places and different stages of decomposition-but all raised by the almighty power of God through Jesus Christ.

In all these cases, the person was raised from the dead to live on the earth and then presumably to die again. How different was the resurrection of the Lord Jesus Christ! He rose, never to die again. His own words are crystal clear: "Fear not; I am the First and the Last, and the Living One; and I was dead, and behold, I am alive for evermore" (Revelation 1:17,18). He is the ever-living One-alive unto the ages of the ages. The epistle to the Hebrews also emphasises this truth in connection with His work as High Priest - "a Priest for ever", "He abideth for ever", "He ever liveth", "After the power of an endless life", "a Son, perfected for evermore". In this respect, as in others, He is the "Firstborn of the dead", "The Firstborn from the dead" and the "First-fruits of them that are asleep". Those that are Christ's at His coming shall "ever be with the Lord". They shall be with Him-always, throughout all eternity.

There is a fundamental difference, however, between the body of Jesus Christ before His resurrection and the bodies of believers before theirs. Christ's body saw no corruption (Acts 2:27); it knew no decay or decomposition. His death was a dissolution of body, soul and spirit, but all the bodily parts continued in the same condition. The corpse was deposited in the tomb belonging to Joseph of Arimathea, but the grave had no power over it. In the case of believers' bodies, it is a very different matter. These corrupt and decay; the bodies, after the spirits and souls have departed, are left to all the sad effects of the grave. The tabernacle or bodily frame is dissolved and generally crumbles into dust, mingling with the dust of the earth.

To Him for whom nothing is too difficult and whose every word is full of power, the resurrection even in these circumstances will provide no difficulties. As the all-powerful and all-knowing God, the Lord Jesus Christ "shall fashion anew the body of our humiliation, that it may be conformed to the body of His glory". By what power will this be effected? "According to the working whereby He is able even to subject ah things unto Himself" (Philippians 3:21).

STUDIES ON THE RESURRECTION OF CHRIST

The resurrection of Christ and the resurrection of the dead are so closely associated that they hold or fall together. Because Christ is the Resurrection, believers shall be resurrected: because He is the Life, they shall live. His life is ours by vital union with Him. His rising from the grave guarantees the rising of all who trust in Him. He is the Firstfruits of all His own who have fallen asleep, the pledge of a great harvest of all believers. He was raised first, thus becoming the Pioneer and Guarantor of those "that are Christ's, at His coming".

Paul the apostle, through the Holy Spirit, stresses this. "If there is no resurrection of the dead, neither hath Christ been raised" (1 Corinthians 15:13). If this were true, the whole basis of the triumph of Christ is taken away. The Christian witness and position would be removed, as Paul continues to elaborate.

(1) "Then is our preaching vain." It would amount to nothing. All the zeal, the missionary endeavour, the patient suffering and self-sacrifice would be to no purpose.

(2) "Your faith also is vain." It would be devoid of truth, unfounded, mere delusion.

(3) "We are found false witnesses of God." Paul and his associates would be guilty of misrepresenting God, if Christ had not been raised.

(4) "Ye are yet in your sins." Still under the control and penalty of sin, without forgiveness.

(5) "They also which are fallen asleep in Christ have perished." Those who died in union with Christ lost!

(6) "We are of all men most pitiable." Miserable themselves and to be pitied by others, they would be of all people the most unfortunate - crucified to this world and vainly hoping for another!

Having thus developed in detail and with force his argument against some of the Corinthian saints who flatly denied the doctrine of the resurrection of the dead, Paul makes it his business to state triumphantly, "But now hath Christ been raised from the dead the firstfruits of them that are asleep" (v.20). To him the resurrection of Christ was an incontestable fact, and the natural corollary of it was the resurrection of His own. Then he proceeds to answer some relevant questions.

"How are the dead raised?" By what means? What power is equal to this effect? They are raised by the quickening power of God. Those who die in Christ are awaiting the reveille of that trumpet which shall sound at Christ's coming. In a moment, they shall be roused and raised. "Remember Jesus Christ, risen from the dead ... Faithful is the saying: For if we died with Him, we shall also live with Him" (2 Timothy 2:8,11).

"With what manner of body do they come?" The body is raised: that is, there is real continuity. But there will also be a difference - it will be a spiritual body. The body of our humiliation will be fashioned anew, and conformed to the body of His glory.

"True the silent grave is keeping

Many a seed in weakness sown;

But the saints in Thee now sleeping,

Raised in power shall share Thy throne;

Resurrection!

Lord of glory, 'tis Thine own."

A seed that is sown differs immensely from the plant that springs up from the ground, but there is undoubtedly oneness and continuity. "The beauty and glory of that which springs up are immeasurably greater than of that which was sown. So the resurrection body of man, in startling contrast to his present body, will be imperishable, glorious, powerful, spiritual, and everlastingly stamped with the image of our Heavenly Saviour" (P.B. Hughes). Then, all weariness and infirmity will be unknown. The believer will be lifted above the passions and prejudices, the wants and weakness of human nature, to enjoy the unwearied vigour of a spiritual body. He shall obtain the promised inheritance and enter into the fullness of His Master's joy.

"But then His face in glory bright

Shall fill our wondering, ravished sight,

And we like Him shall be!

Like Him in all those lovely traits,

Which in His lowly, earthly days

So beautiful we see."

"Freed from all possibility of death, sin and sorrow; filled with all conceivable and inconceivable fulness of happiness; confirmed in an absolute security of an eternal enjoyment; and so they shall continue with God and with the Lamb for evermore." (Dr. J. Pearson).

Those who are "in Christ" are already redeemed by the precious blood of Christ. Yet they wait for the redemption of the body (Romans 8:23). "Having also believed, ye were sealed with the Holy Spirit of promise, which is an earnest of our inheritance, unto the redemption of God's own possession, unto the praise of His glory" (Ephesians 1:13,14). Let us thank God for the indwelling Holy Spirit, our earnest and seal unto the day of redemption!

It is our joy, as those "in Christ", to say with David the Psalmist, "As for me, I shall behold Thy face in righteousness: I shall be satisfied, when I awake, with Thy likeness" (Psalm 17:15).

"Where no shade nor stain can enter,

Nor the gold be dim;

In that holiness unsullied,

I shall walk with Him;

Meet companion for the Master,

From Him, for Him made,

Glory of God's grace for ever,

There in me displayed!"

Did you love *Studies on the Resurrection of Christ*? Then you should read *The Hidden Christ - Volumes 1-4 Box Set* by Hayes Press!

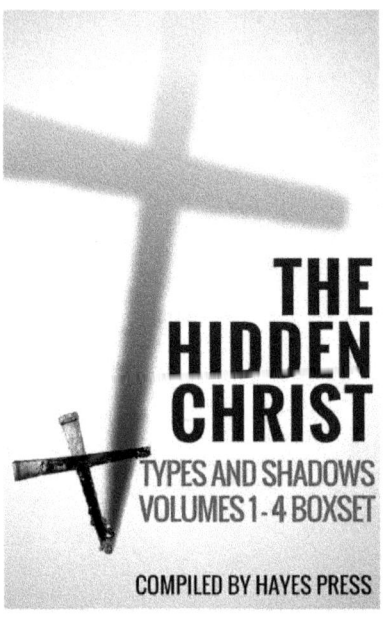

This boxset comprises four previously published volumes, each of which explore some of the many pictures of Jesus Christ that God deliberately hid in the Old Testament:Volume 1: Old Testament (including a focus on the garments of the High Priest)Volume 2: Offerings and SacrificesVolume 3: GenesisVolume 4: Israel's Tabernacle

Also by Hayes Press

Needed Truth
Needed Truth 1888
Needed Truth 2001
Needed Truth 2002
Needed Truth 2003
Needed Truth 2004
Needed Truth 2005
Needed Truth 2006
Needed Truth 2007
Needed Truth 2008
Needed Truth 2009
Needed Truth 2010
Needed Truth 2011
Needed Truth 2012
Needed Truth 2015
Needed Truth 1888-1988: A Centenary Review of Major Themes

Standalone

The Road Through Calvary: 40 Devotional Readings
Lovers of God's House
Different Discipleship: Jesus' Sermon on the Mount
The House of God: Past, Present and Future
The Kingdom of God
Knowing God: His Names and Nature
Churches of God: Their Biblical Constitution and Functions
Four Books About Jesus
Collected Writings On ... Exploring Biblical Fellowship
Collected Writings On ... Exploring Biblical Hope
Collected Writings On ... The Cross of Christ
Builders for God
Collected Writings On ... Exploring Biblical Faithfulness
Collected Writings On ... Exploring Biblical Joy
Possessing the Land: Spiritual Lessons from Joshua
Collected Writings On ... Exploring Biblical Holiness
Collected Writings On ... Exploring Biblical Faith
Collected Writings On ... Exploring Biblical Love
These Three Remain...Exploring Biblical Faith, Hope and Love
The Teaching and Testimony of the Apostles
Pressure Points - Biblical Advice for 20 of Life's Biggest Challenges
More Than a Saviour: Exploring the Person and Work of Jesus
The Psalms: Volumes 1-4 Boxset
The Faith: Outlines of Scripture Doctrine
Key Doctrines of the Christian Gospel
Is There a Purpose to Life?
Bible Covenants 101
The Hidden Christ - Volume 2: Types and Shadows in Offerings and Sacrifices

The Hidden Christ Volume 1: Types and Shadows in the Old Testament
The Hidden Christ - Volume 3: Types and Shadows in Genesis
Heavenly Meanings - The Parables of Jesus
Fisherman to Follower: The Life and Teaching of Simon Peter
Called to Serve: Lessons from the Levites
Needed Truth 2017 Issue 1
The Breaking of the Bread: Its History, Its Observance, Its Meaning
Spiritual Revivals of the Bible
An Introduction to the Book of Hebrews
The Holy Spirit and the Believer
The Psalms: Volume 1 - Thoughts on Key Themes
The Psalms: Volume 2 - Exploring Key Elements
The Psalms: Volume 3 - Surveying Key Sections
The Psalms: Volume 4 - Savouring Choice Selections
Profiles of the Prophets
The Hidden Christ - Volumes 1-4 Box Set
The Hidden Christ - Volume 4: Types and Shadows in Israel's Tabernacle
Baptism - Its Meaning and Teaching
Conflict and Controversy in the Church of God in Corinth
In the Shadow of Calvary: A Bible Study of John 12-17
Moses: God's Deliverer
Sparkling Facets: The Names and Titles of Jesus
A Little Book About Being Christlike
Keys to Church Growth
From Shepherd Boy to Sovereign: The Life of David
Back to Basics: A Guide to Essential Bible Teaching
An Introduction to the Holy Spirit
Israel and the Church in Bible Prophecy

"Growth and Fruit" and Other Writings by John Drain
15 Hot Topics For Today's Christian
Needed Truth Volume 2 1889
Studies on the Return of Christ
Studies on the Resurrection of Christ
Needed Truth Volume 3 1890
The Nations of the Old Testament: Their Relationship with Israel and Bible Prophecy
The Message of the Minor Prophets
Insights from Isaiah
The Bible - Its Inspiration and Authority
Lessons from Ezra and Nehemiah
A Bible Study of God's Names For His People

About the Publisher

Hayes Press (www.hayespress.org) is a registered charity in the United Kingdom, whose primary mission is to disseminate the Word of God, mainly through literature. It is one of the largest distributors of gospel tracts and leaflets in the United Kingdom, with over 100 titles and hundreds of thousands despatched annually. In addition to paperbacks and eBooks, Hayes Press also publishes Plus Eagles Wings, a fun and educational Bible magazine for children, and Golden Bells, a popular daily Bible reading calendar in wall or desk formats. Also available are over 100 Bibles in many different versions, shapes and sizes, Bible text posters and much more!

www.ingramcontent.com/pod-product-compliance
Lightning Source LLC
Chambersburg PA
CBHW071324040426
42444CB00009B/2075